AQA
GCSE

WORKIN... ...OLOGY
Achieve...

Tony Childs

Highly experienced ...

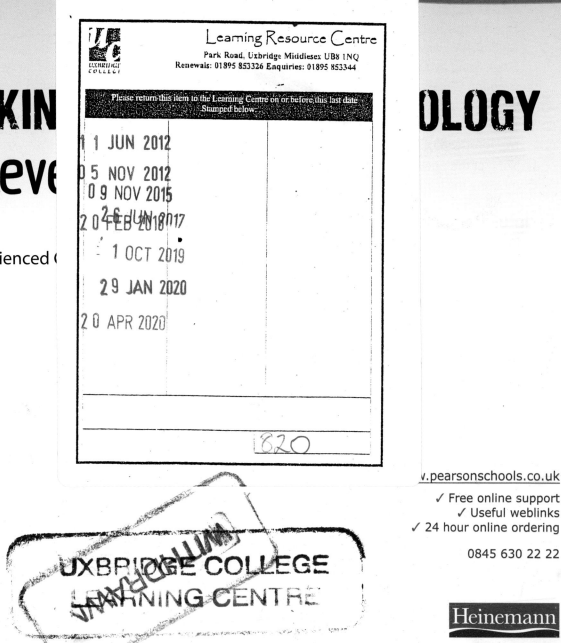

...v.pearsonschools.co.uk

✓ Free online support
✓ Useful weblinks
✓ 24 hour online ordering

0845 630 22 22

Heinemann

Part of Pearson

Contents

Chapter 3: Conflict 62

Chapter 4: Relationships 92

Chapter 5: The unseen poem 122

Chapter 6: Exam practice – make the grade 132

Introduction

How does this book work?

This book is designed to help students raise their achievement in Unit 2 or Unit 5 of the AQA GCSE English Literature specification. It is tailored to the requirements of the specification to help students achieve grades B–A*.

The book breaks the Assessment Objectives down into their component parts. It then provides students with:

▶ guidance and teaching on the key skills that make the difference between a B, A and A* grade

▶ examples of students' work at grades B, A and A* with examiner comments which highlight what is good and what could be improved

▶ activities that allow them to reflect on and improve their learning

▶ the relevant mark scheme descriptors together with guidance on what the examiners are looking for

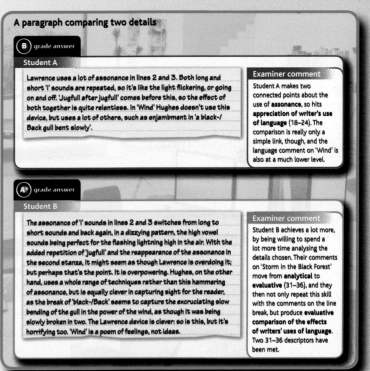

A paragraph comparing two details

B grade answer

Student A

Lawrence uses a lot of assonance in lines 2 and 3. Both long and short 'i' sounds are repeated, so it's like the light flickering, or going on and off. 'Jugfull after jugfull' comes before this, so the effect of both together is quite relentless. In 'Wind' Hughes doesn't use this device, but uses a lot of others, such as enjambment in 'a black-/ Back gull bent slowly'.

Examiner comment

Student A makes two connected points about the use of **assonance**, so hits **appreciation of writer's use of language** (18–24). The comparison is really only a simple link, though, and the language comment on 'Wind' is also at a much lower level.

A* grade answer

Student B

The assonance of 'i' sounds in lines 2 and 3 switches from long to short sounds and back again, in a dizzying pattern, the high vowel sounds being perfect for the flashing lightning high in the air. With the added repetition of 'jugfull' and the reappearance of the assonance in the second stanza, it might seem as though Lawrence is overdoing it; but perhaps that's the point. It is overpowering. Hughes, on the other hand, uses a whole range of techniques rather than this hammering of assonance, but is equally clever in capturing sight for the reader, as the break of 'black-/Back' seems to capture the excruciating slow bending of the gull in the power of the wind, as though it was being slowly broken in two. The Lawrence device is clever, so is this, but it's horrifying too. 'Wind' is a poem of feelings, not ideas.

Examiner comment

Student B achieves a lot more, by being willing to spend a lot more time analysing the details chosen. Their comments on 'Storm in the Black Forest' move from **analytical** to **evaluative** (31–36), and they then not only repeat this skill with the comments on the line break, but produce **evaluative comparison of the effects of writers' uses of language**. Two 31–36 descriptors have been met.

▶ hints from an experienced Chief Examiner on how to move from a B to an A and then to an A*.

The approach that this book uses comes out of many years of examining experience and out of workshops, training sessions and revision courses with teachers and students. It can be used with confidence by all students who have the potential to move from a grade B to an A and then to an A*.

How is the book structured?

The book is broken down into 6 Chapters. Chapters 1–4 cover the poems in the AQA Anthology and the following approach is taken in each of these chapters:

▶ Looking at the poems as a whole.
▶ Looking at the poems individually.
▶ Comparing the poems and writing in the exam.

Each chapter also includes:

▶ an explanation of the relevant Assessment Objectives
▶ learning objectives ('My learning')
▶ activities

▶ glossed words from the poems
▶ contextual explanations
▶ sample answers with examiner comments
▶ opportunities for peer or self-assessment.

Chapter 5 focuses on the Unseen poem and Chapter 6 provides a complete practice exam paper together with mark schemes and explanations.

What do the Assessment Objectives mean?

AO1: in response to the first Assessment Objective you must write about your response to the poems using details from the poems to support your ideas. You can say what you think the poem is about as a whole or what particular details mean, and you should think about how other readers might interpret these details.

AO2: in response to the second Assessment Objective you have to write about the writers' methods and their purposes in using these methods. The methods are broken down into three:

▶ **Language:** the words the writers have chosen to use, their vocabulary, their use of imagery, and so on.
▶ **Structure:** the way the writers have chosen to order their words and ideas either within a whole poem (what have the writers chosen to begin and end the poem with?) or within a stanza or sometimes even within a single line.
▶ **Form:** the particular form of poetry chosen. It can refer to the overall structure chosen, such as sonnet form, or details the writer has chosen, such as rhyme and rhythm.

Although you need to think about all of these things when you work on a poem, you won't necessarily have to write about all of them in the exam. For instance, in the A* descriptor **evaluation of writers' uses of language and/or structure and/or form**, 'and/or' means just that – so an evaluation of language would be enough. However, you must always use details from the poems to support what you are saying and link the technique you're writing about to the meaning you think the writer was trying to convey or its effect on the reader.

AO3: in response to the third Assessment Objective you have to compare both what the poems are about and the ways in which they are written, using details from the poems to support your ideas.

The AQA GCSE English Literature specification

This book is for students taking Unit 2 or Unit 5 of the AQA GCSE English Literature specification. Unit 2 offers students the opportunity to be assessed on the poetry requirements in an exam. Unit 5 offers the poetry assessment as Controlled Assessment. The principal focus of this book is on Unit 2. However, students taking Unit 5 will find most of the content of this book relevant and helpful.

An overview of the full GCSE specification for English Literature, including the requirements for Unit 5, can be found in the corresponding Heinemann Teacher Guide or on the AQA website.

GCSE English Literature Unit 2

Here is an overview of the Unit 2 exam. This book is principally designed to support this unit.

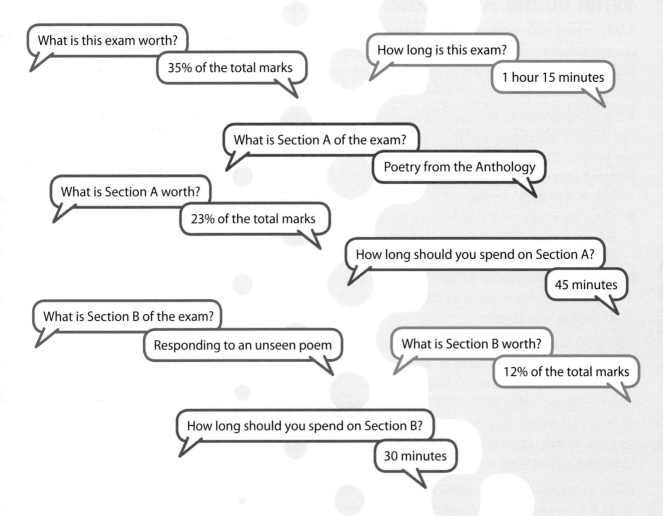

What is this exam worth?

35% of the total marks

How long is this exam?

1 hour 15 minutes

What is Section A of the exam?

Poetry from the Anthology

What is Section A worth?

23% of the total marks

How long should you spend on Section A?

45 minutes

What is Section B of the exam?

Responding to an unseen poem

What is Section B worth?

12% of the total marks

How long should you spend on Section B?

30 minutes

For full details, see the corresponding Teacher Guide and AQA specification.

AQA GCSE English Literature: further resources from Pearson Education

▶ Teacher Guide – full colour 'visual' lesson plans can be found in the corresponding Heinemann Teacher Guide, written by experienced author and Head of English, David Grant. These lesson plans also make suggestions about how to incorporate materials from the AQA Digital Anthology. Full support for the Controlled Assessment requirements is also included, written by Steve Davies.

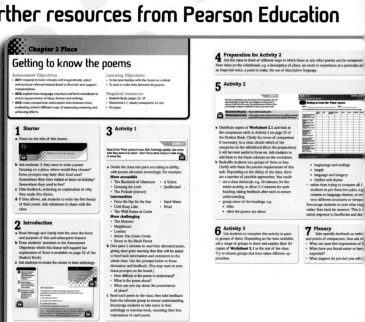

▶ Heinemann and Longman set texts – the AQA specification prescribes Heinemann and Longman editions of several set texts. For details of the widest available range of hardback educational editions, see our website or catalogue.

▶ Heinemann ActiveTeach for *Of Mice and Men* and *An Inspector Calls* – exciting new ActiveTeach versions of the two most popular set texts, available as educational e-books exclusively from Pearson Education. In addition to an electronic copy of the text that corresponds to our educational edition you will find a wealth of resources to help students engage with and understand the text, as well as a bank of activities focused on grade improvement.

My learning ▶

In this section you will learn how to:
- become familiar with the poems as a whole
- start to make links between the poems.

Getting to know the poems

The poems

The Clown Punk *Simon Armitage*	**Brendon Gallacher** *Jackie Kay*	**The River God** *Stevie Smith*
Checking Out Me History *John Agard*	**Give** *Simon Armitage*	**The Hunchback in the Park** *Dylan Thomas*
Horse Whisperer *Andrew Forster*	**Les Grands Seigneurs** *Dorothy Molloy*	**The Ruined Maid** *Thomas Hardy*
Medusa *Carol Ann Duffy*	**Ozymandias** *Percy Bysshe Shelley*	**Casehistory: Alison (head injury)** *U.A. Fanthorpe*
Singh Song *Daljit Nagra*	**My Last Duchess** *Robert Browning*	**On a Portrait of a Deaf Man** *John Betjeman*

Assessment Objectives:

AO1 respond to texts critically and imaginatively; select and evaluate relevant textual detail to illustrate and support interpretations.

AO2 explain how language, structure and form contribute to writers' presentation of ideas, themes and settings.

AO3 make comparisons and explain links between texts, evaluating writers' different ways of expressing meaning and achieving effects.

Introduction

The poems in this chapter are centred around character and voice. Learning how a poet uses character and voice is a key part of enjoying and analysing poetry. All the poems are in your AQA Anthology.

In this chapter you will be:

▶ looking at the individual poems

▶ comparing the poems

▶ learning how to approach exam questions.

As a result of this preparation you will be developing your writing skills in order to hit the Assessment Objectives. See page v for more information about what the Assessment Objectives mean. In the exam you will have to compare two poems from this chapter.

Getting started

The first thing to do is to start to familiarise yourself with the 'Character and voice' poems. You can do the following activities by yourself, or in a group.

Activity 1

Read all the 'Character and voice' poems in your AQA Anthology, quickly. Just notice what they seem to be about – don't worry about trying to make sense of every line.

Activity 2

Now find as many links as you can between some of the poems. You will need a large piece of paper with some headings on. Below is a list of ways you could look at the poems. You could use some of these to form your headings, though you could think of some of your own as well.

Ways to look at the poems	Tips on what to watch out for
What the poems are about	Look for general ideas here, such as death, birth, memory, relationship between parent and child. Make a note of poems that seem to have some meanings in common.
Beginnings/endings	Any similarities? How about lines that look similar, but where there's a difference too? For example, both 'Medusa' and 'Casehistory: Alison' end with single lines, separated from the rest of the poem, but they have very different effects on the reader. Think of as many differences as you can.
Length	You might notice some distinct similarities or differences. Include the number and length of **stanzas**, if there are any.
Rhyme	You need to look a little more carefully now. Is there a regular **rhyme scheme**? Does it change? Be careful – some poems that don't seem to rhyme often use a lot of **half-rhyme** or **echoes**, or might suddenly rhyme. Look at 'The Clown Punk', for example. There are a lot of half-rhymes, but only one full rhyme, in the last two lines. If you were working on this poem, you'd need to think about why the writer does this.
Rhythm	'Checking Out Me History' is one poem that has a strong **rhythm**. Can you find others?
Language	Some poems in this chapter are older than others, and some might use non-standard forms of English. Look for ones that are similar, and ones that are very different. For example, 'The Ruined Maid' uses some nineteenth-century rural English, whereas 'Checking Out Me History' uses Caribbean English.
Imagery	Some poems are rich in **imagery** such as **metaphors** and **similes**, whereas others might seem quite plain. Make a note of some obvious similarities and differences.

Now that you have found a lot of links, try displaying your findings in a different way, on a sheet of A3 paper. Working on your own, in a pair or in a group, you could try any of the following ways.

1   Spread the titles out on the sheet and draw links between them, labelling each one.

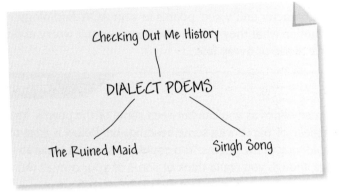

2   Draw a picture or symbol for each idea (such as death or nature) that appears in more than one poem, and group the poems around each – a poem can appear in more than one group.

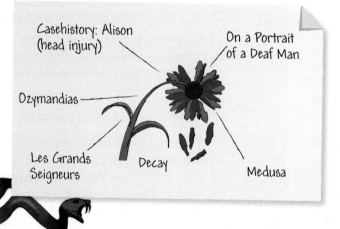

3   Draw a picture, or pictures, for each poem on the sheet, and link similar ones with arrows.

In these activities you have started to tackle all three Assessment Objectives. Now you will be focusing on AO1 and AO2 as you look at the poems individually (pages 5–21). You will return to AO3 when you compare the poems (pages 22–25). Finally, you will look at how to turn your knowledge and skills into successful exam answers, before you attempt one yourself (pages 26–31).

Looking at the poems individually

Looking at the poems individually

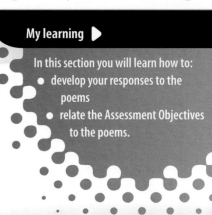

My learning ▶

In this section you will learn how to:
- develop your responses to the poems
- relate the Assessment Objectives to the poems.

This section of the chapter, pages 5–21, is designed to lead you through an exploration of each individual poem. Throughout, you will find examples of student responses at different levels.

In the exam, you will have to write about the poems individually as well as comparing them.

In the exam you have to compare two poems; one named poem and one unnamed, which means you can choose the second one. On the Higher Tier paper the following will not be named poems: 'Brendon Gallacher', 'Give', 'The Ruined Maid'. Of course, you could choose any of these poems to compare with the named one.

Assessment Objectives:

The Assessment Objectives you will be focusing on in this part of the chapter are:

AO1 respond to texts critically and imaginatively; select and evaluate relevant textual detail to illustrate and support interpretations.

AO2 explain how language, structure and form contribute to writers' presentation of ideas, themes and settings.

The Clown Punk

by Simon Armitage

Read the poem in your AQA Anthology, then complete the activities below.

GradeStudio

Examiner tip

Poetic devices
In the exam, you should refer to poetic devices such as **metaphor** or **simile**, and other terms, carefully and correctly. Terms in **bold** are explained in the Glossary of Poetic Devices (page 137).

▶ **Poem Glossary**

shonky   dirty, derelict

GradeStudio

Sample answer Ⓑ

To achieve a B on this AO2 descriptor, you need to show **appreciation and consideration of writers' uses of language and/or form and/or structure**. To do this, you need to do more than just explain an effect. The following extract from a sample answer would hit the grade B requirement.

> Activity 1, question 1a
> Comparing the punk to 'a basket of washing' is quite funny, because the image of a walking basket towing a dog is amusing, but it also makes him seem untidy and chaotic.

Initial responses

Activity 1

1   What details tell you that the clown punk is poor?
  a   What things does the writer compare the punk to?
  b   Do these comparisons make him seem less than human? How?
2   Why might the children 'wince and scream' at the clown punk?
3   How does the writer convey the effects of age on the clown punk?
4   There are a lot of references to colour in the poem. Find as many as you can, and comment on the effects that they have.
5   Look at the **rhymes** in the poem. A lot of them are loose, but the last two lines rhyme fully, so that a lot of stress falls on 'rain' and the connection with 'brain'. Think of as many reasons as you can for this.
6   What do you think the writer wants you to feel about the clown punk at the end of the poem? Why do you think this?
7   What is the attitude of the **speaker** to the clown punk? Don't just think about the last two lines – think about what else the speaker reveals about himself.

Words/phrases to explore (AO1 and AO2)

Activity 2

1   Bearing in mind what you've found in answering the questions in Activity 1, look at the last line of the poem: what does each word connect with in the rest of the poem?
2   Think carefully about the phrase 'let it rain'. How many effects of this phrase can you think of, bearing in mind that these are the last three words?

Comparing with other poems

Activity 3

1   **Comparing ideas and themes**
   Compare the attitudes to a disadvantaged person in 'The Clown Punk' and 'The Hunchback in the Park'.
2   **Comparing writers' devices**
   Compare the ways that language and stanza change at the end of 'The Clown Punk' and 'Les Grands Seigneurs'.

Checking Out Me History

by John Agard

Read the poem in your AQA Anthology, then complete the activities below.

Initial responses

Activity 1

1 This poem is all about the history that people are told about, often in school, and other history that we might not know about. Find examples in the poem of the following things that people do learn in school:
- real events
- characters from children's stories
- nursery **rhymes**.

2 'Dem never tell me bout dat'. Which people and events has the **speaker** not been told about?

3 Look at the **stanzas** about Toussaint, Nanny and Mary Seacole.
  a Pick out all the words that suggest the speaker's admiration of the characters, such as 'beacon'.
  b Why do you think the writer has chosen to use short lines in these stanzas?

4 Look at the stanza about Nanny.
  a Which words suggest that she is almost a mythical figure? Which words suggest something real?
  b Why do you think the writer refers to her as a 'fire-woman' and compares her to a 'stream' and a 'river'?

5 In the stanza about Mary Seacole there is a simple triple rhyme: 'go/no/snow'. How does the writer change the **tone** in the four lines that follow, beginning 'a healing star'? Think about language and line length.

Words/phrases to explore (AO1 and AO2)

Activity 2

Now you've explored the poem, think again about the word 'Dem'. Agard begins the poem with 'Dem tell me', and repeats it at the beginning of the last stanza.
a Who are 'dem' by the end of the poem, do you think?
b What effects do the last two lines have?

Comparing with other poems

Activity 3

1 **Comparing ideas and themes**
Compare the attitudes to history in 'Checking Out Me History' and 'Horse Whisperer'.

2 **Comparing writers' devices**
Compare the ways in which the writers use repetition in 'Checking Out Me History' and 'Brendon Gallacher'.

GradeStudio

Contexts

Toussaint L'Ouverture was a Haitian revolutionary leader. Born a slave, he fought against French, Spanish and British forces at different times and was credited with establishing Haiti's independence.

Nanny de Maroon was the spiritual leader of the Windward Maroons and a brilliant military strategist. She directed an effective resistance movement against the British.

Shaka was a great leader of the Zulu people in South Africa.

The Caribs and Arawaks were among the Caribbean people whose islands were taken over after the Europeans arrived in 1492.

Mary Seacole was a nurse of mixed race who helped wounded and dying British soldiers at the front in the Crimean war against Russia.

GradeStudio

Sample answer B

To achieve a B on this AO1 descriptor, you need to show **details linked to interpretation**. To do this, you need to link details to your view of what the poem is about. The following extract from a sample answer would hit the grade B requirement.

> **Activity 1, question 3a**
> The speaker clearly regards the 'hidden' historical figures as heroic. This is shown by the words he uses to describe them, such as 'vision', 'see-far', 'freedom' and 'sunrise'.

Horse Whisperer

by Andrew Forster

Read the poem in your AQA Anthology, then complete the activities below.

GradeStudio

Sample answer Ⓐ

To achieve an A on this AO2 descriptor, you need to show **analysis of the writers' uses of language and/or structure and/or form and their effect on the reader**. To do this, you need to look carefully at a choice that the writer has made. The following extract from a sample answer would hit the grade A requirement.

> The line 'The searing breath, the glistening veins' brings the horses vividly alive: 'searing' and 'glistening' are present participles which suggest action now, so clear is the memory for the whisperer, and the rhythm of the line lifts these words out. These are qualities that could only be seen by someone in close contact with the animals.

Initial responses

Activity 1

1 What is the **speaker's** attitude to horses? Look carefully at everything that she says and thinks about them. There is more than one thing that you can say.
2 How does the speaker see herself? What sort of character does she think she is?
3 Bearing in mind what you have found in answering the two questions above, how would you assess her character?
4 Why do you think the whisperer's 'secret' in the first **stanza** worked?
5 What was the 'legacy of whispers' do you think?
6 What change is mentioned in the third stanza? Why do you think it leads to the whisperers being driven out?
7 Which word in the fourth stanza suggests the whisperer's affinity with the horses?

Words/phrases to explore (AO1 and AO2)

Activity 2

Look at the end of the poem. How does the writer create a sense of the life of the horses by the words he uses here? Look at the type of words he uses, the repetition of sound and **rhythm**, and the effect of the last line.

Comparing with other poems

Activity 3

1 **Comparing ideas and themes**
Compare the situations of the central characters in 'Horse Whisperer' and 'The Hunchback in the Park'.
2 **Comparing writers' devices**
Compare the ways in which the writers establish character in 'Horse Whisperer' and 'My Last Duchess'.

Medusa

by Carol Ann Duffy

Read the poem in your AQA Anthology, then complete the activities below.

GradeStudio

Context

Medusa In Greek mythology Medusa was a Gorgon, a creature whose gaze turned onlookers to stone. She was the only mortal Gorgon, and the goddess Athena turned Medusa's hair into snakes when she found her lying in her temple with Poseidon. She was killed by Perseus, who avoided her gaze by looking at her in a mirror rather than directly.

Activity 1

Initial responses

1 Carol Ann Duffy takes the story of Medusa and imagines her as an ageing woman. What references to the Greek myth described above can you find in the poem?

2 In the first **stanza**, what is it that turns her hair into snakes? How does Duffy make Medusa's thoughts seem like snakes?

3 In the second stanza, Duffy makes the woman seem ageing and dangerous. How? Look at the words and what they suggest as well as what they say directly.

4 **a** Why should the man be 'terrified' that Medusa loves him?
   b Why is it better for her 'if you were stone'?

5 Why is the result of the Gorgon's stare apt for each of the animals in stanzas four and five?

6 Look at the end of the poem.
   a How has the man changed from the one Medusa loved, do you think?
   b Find the repetitions of words and phrases. What do they convey about Medusa's state of mind?
   c What meanings does the last line have? What is the effect of placing it on a separate line?

Activity 2

Words/phrases to explore (AO1)

Now you've explored the poem, find the phrase in it that best sums up Medusa's state of mind. Make sure that you can find more than one reason for your choice.

Activity 3

Comparing with other poems

1 **Comparing ideas and themes**
   Compare the attitudes to men in 'Medusa' and 'Les Grands Seigneurs'.

2 **Comparing writers' devices**
   Compare the effects of the ways the endings are written in 'Medusa' and 'Les Grands Seigneurs'.

GradeStudio

Sample answer B

To achieve a B on this AO2 descriptor, you need to show **appreciation/consideration of writers' uses of language and/ or structure and/or form and their effect on readers**. To do this, you need to say at least two things about a writer's choice. The following extract from a sample answer would hit the grade B requirement.

> Activity 1, question 6c
> The last line being on its own makes the threat seem immediate, and the last word 'now' makes the reader imagine the end of the poem is the moment when he turns to stone.

Singh Song

by Daljit Nagra

Read the poem in your AQA Anthology, then complete the activities below.

Initial responses

1   Although there are other voices in the poem, the main voice is Singh's. What does the poem reveal about his life? Think about:
   • what he has to do   • how he is treated by other people.
2   What is revealed about Singh's character? Think about:
   • his response to other people   • his attitude to his bride.
3   What is revealed about Singh's bride? Think about:
   • what she does   • her appearance   • her attitude to other people.
4   Look at the **stanza** beginning 'Late in de midnight hour'. Which words and phrases suggest an atmosphere of romance here, and which words and phrases seem to show the opposite?
5   Look at the conversation between Singh and his bride. How are their words typical of each of them?
6   Nagra gives the last line to Singh. What is the effect of this line?
7   The voice in the poem speaks in Indian English. Which words do you think are **dialect words** (words from a specific region), rather than the writer just showing accent (how the words are spoken)?

Words/phrases to explore (AO1)

'Is priceless baby –' says Singh in the last line. How is Singh's life split between money and romance, and which do you think is more important to him?

Comparing with other poems

1   **Comparing ideas and themes**
   Compare the attitudes to women in 'Singh Song' and 'My Last Duchess'.
2   **Comparing writers' devices**
   Compare the ways in which the **speaker's** voice is created in 'Singh Song' and 'The River God'.

GradeStudio

Sample answer Ⓐ

To achieve an A on this AO2 descriptor, you need to show **exploration of ideas/themes**. To do this, you need to have several ideas about the poem. The following extract from a sample answer would hit the grade A requirement.

> Activity 1, question 1
> In some ways Singh appears to have a miserable life: he is forced by his 'daddy' to work long hours, and he is abused by his customers in his down-at-heel shop. His 'newly bride' seems a bit of a monster, who abuses his parents. On the other hand, he shuts his shop when he wants to, and loves his wife with a hopeless romanticism. He seems to be a hopeless shopkeeper too, though: the state of the shop seems to be his fault.

Brendon Gallacher

by Jackie Kay

Read the poem in your AQA Anthology,
then complete the activities below.

Initial responses

Activity 1

1   The name 'Brendon Gallacher' is like a **refrain** in this
    poem – it recurs from the title onwards. Why do you think
    the writer includes it three times in the opening **stanza**?

2   The first stanza is about family. Think about the differences
    between the **speaker's** family and Brendon Gallacher. What
    reasons can you find here for the speaker creating Brendon?

3   In the first stanza the writer creates a contrast between the
    speaker's family and Brendon's by balancing the two as she writes.
    The first is 'He was seven and I was six.' Find as many other
    balances like this as you can in the stanza.

4   What clue does the first line of the second stanza give for another
    possible reason for the child inventing Brendon?

5   'how his mum drank and his daddy was a cat burglar.' Why do you
    think the child creates this?

6   What additional qualities in Brendon that might appeal to the
    speaker are mentioned in the last stanza? Do they suggest anything
    about the speaker?

7   What is the effect of the repetitions in the last line?

Words/phrases to explore (AO2)
Activity 2

The line 'how his mum drank and his daddy was a cat burglar' sounds
like a child speaking, even though the poem is in the voice of an older
person looking back. How does the writer create the language and
thoughts of a child? Look for sentence forms as well as vocabulary.

Comparing with other poems
Activity 3

1   **Comparing ideas and themes**
    Compare the central characters in 'Brendon Gallacher' and 'On a
    Portrait of a Deaf Man'.

2   **Comparing writers' devices**
    Compare the ways in which the writers create sympathy for the
    speakers in 'Brendon Gallacher' and 'On a Portrait of a Deaf Man'.

GradeStudio

Sample answer B

To achieve a B on this AO2
descriptor, you need to show
**appreciation of writers' uses
of language and/or structure
and/or form and their effect on
readers.** To do this, you need to
offer more than one idea about
effect. The following extract from
a sample answer would hit the
grade B requirement.

> Activity I, question 7
> The repeated 'Oh' on
> the last line of the poem,
> together with the final
> repetition of 'Brendon
> Gallacher', creates a
> real sense of sorrow and
> loss as the final effect,
> especially with 'Brendon'
> used just as a first name
> for the first time in the
> poem, which makes it
> seem even more of a
> personal loss.

Give

by Simon Armitage

Read the poem in your AQA Anthology, then complete the activities below.

Initial responses

Answer the following questions:

1 Who do you think the beggar is speaking to? Try to think of more than one possibility, and then check through the poem to see if the beggar's words make sense for each possibility.

2 What does the other person think of the beggar? Base your response on details from the poem.

3 Does the beggar resent having to beg? How do you know?

4 The beggar seems desperate. How is this conveyed to the reader? Look at the middle of the poem, not just the end, and trace the way the voice moves from one thing to the next.

5 There are a lot of patterns in this poem. Work out the word and **rhyme** patterning in the first four lines. How does it lead to the two words 'here' and 'yours', and why to these two words?

6 Now look at the last two lines. Look at the patterns of rhymes and **half-rhymes** here – not just at the end of the lines. Why has the poet decided to finish with four short sentences? Think about the effect that has built up by the time you reach the last sentence.

Words/phrases to explore (AO1)

Look again at line 10. How many possible meanings can you find here?

Comparing with other poems

1 **Comparing ideas and themes**
Compare the attitudes of the voices in 'Give' and 'Medusa' to the person they are speaking to.

2 **Comparing writers' devices**
Compare the writing of the last two lines of 'The Clown Punk' with the last two lines of 'Give'. Look at the length of the sentences, the effects of the full stops and the rhymes, the effects of the last four words of each poem.

Les Grands Seigneurs

by Dorothy Molloy

Read the poem in your AQA Anthology, then complete the activities below.

Initial responses

Activity 1

1 In the first two **stanzas**, the **speaker** makes fourteen comparisons with men.

   a The first two lines contain comparisons to architectural features, like towers. There are three more types of comparisons that the speaker makes. Decide what they are.

   b Some of the things she uses have different levels of meaning. For example, 'nightingales' have a beautiful song, but also sing mainly at night – perhaps she values what they do at night. Choose two more comparisons that might have a hidden meaning beneath the superficial meaning, and explore them.

2 In the third stanza the speaker thinks about herself.

   a In the first line and a half, how does she see the relationship that she used to have with men?

   b Looking back at the first two stanzas, which of the items she mentions belong specifically to the past?

3 The last stanza changes everything.

   a How is the change signalled in the first line?

   b How is the language of the stanza now modern instead of old? Look for sentence and phrase forms as well as individual words.

   c Looking back to the third stanza, which phrase suggests that this is a modern woman, not a woman who is actually from history?

   d Look at the list of things that she 'became'. What do all of these things imply about the relationship now?

   e Why did the change happen 'overnight'?

Words/phrases to explore (AO1)

Activity 2

Look again at the last word of the poem.

1 What do you think the speaker means by her 'bluff'? Think what this might imply about her attitude to herself, to her husband, and to men in general.

2 How do you feel about it?

Comparing with other poems

Activity 3

1 **Comparing ideas and themes**
   Compare the attitudes to men in 'Medusa' and 'Les Grands Seigneurs'.

2 **Comparing writers' devices**
   Compare the ways in which voice is created in 'Les Grands Seigneurs' and 'My Last Duchess'.

▶ Poem Glossary

buttresses/castellated towers architectural features of old castles

hurdy-gurdy man a hurdy-gurdy was a musical instrument worked with a crank. The hurdy-gurdy man went through the streets, asking for money

courtly love a medieval concept of chivalry and love. Part of this tradition was the songs sung by **troubadours**

GradeStudio

Sample answer Ⓐ✱

To achieve an A* on this AO1 descriptor, you need to show **insightful exploratory response to text**. The following extract from a sample answer would hit the grade A* requirement.

> **Activity 2, question 1**
> The last word, 'bluff', seems to imply that all of her previous attitudes were mere posturing, that the reality, the truth behind the 'bluff', is that she really is just 'a plaything' for this man, or for men in general. Having role-played at 'courtly love', she now recognises that in the modern world the situation is reversed, with men firmly in control, commanding and denigrating women. This woman is lost.

Context

Ozymandias was another name for Rameses, one of the Egyptian pharaohs.

Ozymandias
by Percy Bysshe Shelley

Read the poem in your AQA Anthology, then complete the activities below.

Initial responses

1 Find the adjectives in lines 2 and 4. How does each of them add to the effect of the whole poem?
2 What do the ends of line 4 and line 5 suggest about the nature of the king? How is this added to in lines 9–11?
3 The remains of the statue are 'lifeless'. Does the word have more than one meaning here?
4 'Look on my works, ye Mighty, and despair!' What did this mean when it was written, and what does it mean in the **context** of the poem?
5 Line 12 begins 'Nothing beside remains.' This is the shortest sentence in the poem.
   a Why do you think Shelley has used such a short sentence?
   b Why do you think he has placed it after the previous thought, and at the beginning of a line?
   c What makes the thought here seem so definite?
6 Find the adjectives in the last two lines. What do they emphasise?
7 What effects does the last line have? Think about:
   • the adjectives
   • the **rhythm** of the line
   • the meanings of the last three words – how are they similar?

Words/phrases to explore (AO1 and AO2)

At the beginning of the poem is the traveller 'from an antique land'. Why do you think the place is 'antique', and why isn't Shelley more exact about the place?

Comparing with other poems

1 **Comparing ideas and themes**
   Compare the central characters in 'Ozymandias' and 'My Last Duchess'.
2 **Comparing writers' devices**
   Compare the ways that character is created in 'Ozymandias' and 'My Last Duchess'.

Sample answer Ⓐ

To achieve an A on this AO2 descriptor, you need to show **analytical use of detail to support interpretation**. To do this, you need to look closely at some supporting detail. You need to say at least two things about a writer's choice. The following extract from a sample answer would hit the grade A requirement.

> **Activity 1, question 6**
> The adjectives in the last two lines stress both the size of the statue (and by inference the king), and the finality of the fall: the wreck is 'colossal' and the sands 'boundless' and 'level': 'nothing' is left of the mighty kingdom.

My Last Duchess
by Robert Browning

Read the poem in your AQA
Anthology, then complete the
activities below.

GradeStudio
Contexts
Ferrara a duchy in northern Italy.
The Duke is probably based on
Alfonso, whose wife Lucrezia died
in 1561 at the age of 17.
**Frà Pandolf/Claus of
Innsbruck** these two artists are
probably fictional.

Initial responses

Activity 1

1 This poem is a **dramatic monologue**, a poem in which the
speaker reveals things about himself which he may or may not
know. A lot is revealed through the Duchess here.
  a What facts do we learn about the Duchess in the poem?
  b What do other people think about the Duchess?
  c Now look again at what the Duke thinks of her. What does he
     disapprove of in her words and actions? What do these things
     reveal about her, and about him?
2 The poem is written in **iambic pentameter**, so that every second
  syllable is stressed. Say lines 9, 10 and 11 aloud, making sure you
  stress the second syllable in each pair. What does this reveal about
  the Duke's view of himself?
3 Look at lines 33–43. What other examples can you find of the
  Duke's view of himself?
4 In line 46, what is the effect of the line break after the phrase
  'There she stands'?
5 The Duke stops looking at the portrait after 'As if alive' (line 47).
  What do you learn about the Duke after this point? How does that
  affect the reader's view of him?
6 Look carefully at the last sentence.
  a Why is this particular statue mentioned here? What does it
     suggest about the Duke and his relationship with his wife?
  b Say the last line out loud again, and notice the effect of the
     stresses. Which word in particular stands out, and why?

Words/phrases to explore (AO1)

Activity 2

Now you've explored the poem, think again about the Duke's comment
when he mentions Frà Pandolf 'by design'. How does the Duke speak
and act 'by design'?

Comparing with other poems

Activity 3

1 **Comparing ideas and themes**
  Compare the characters and situations of the duchess in 'My Last
  Duchess' and the central character in 'Les Grands Seigneurs'.
2 **Comparing writers' devices**
  Compare the ways in which voice is created in 'My Last Duchess'
  and 'The River God'.

GradeStudio
Sample answer Ⓐ
To achieve an A* on this AO2
descriptor, you need to show
**evaluation of writers' uses of
language and/or structure
and/or form and their effect
on readers**. To do this, you need
to analyse some detail closely
and evaluate its effect. The
following extract from a sample
answer would hit the grade A*
requirement.

Activity I, question 6a
The Duke's arrogance is
summed up by his choice
of subject for the statue
made 'for me'. He chooses
Neptune, a violent god with
a vicious trident, shown
taming a sea horse. The
reader cannot help seeing
the Duke in Neptune, and
his unfortunate wife as the
sea horse – a wild and
beautiful creature, admired
by civilised people but
ruthlessly destroyed by a
figure who believes himself
superior and untouchable.
The psychopath stands
revealed.

The River God

by Stevie Smith

Read the poem in your AQA Anthology, then complete the activities below.

Initial responses

1 How does the writer make the voice seem like a god? Look at the attitudes the voice has, and the words it uses.
2 What sort of character does the god seem to be to you? Think about what he enjoys, his attitude to the woman, what he thinks of himself, and the words he uses to convey these attitudes.
3 The river god is a spirit of water.
   a Find as many references to water and rivers as you can.
   b Which words sound like water, or the effect of water?
   c Which of the words you have found are the most effective in saying something about the god?
4 Look at the **rhymes** in the poem.
   a The **rhyme scheme** changes at the end. What is the effect of 'bed' and 'head' rhyming, do you think?
   b 'Head' and 'her' do not rhyme. Why do you think Smith chose not to rhyme the last two lines? What effect does it have?
5 Look at the repetitions and exclamations in the poem. What effects do they have?
6 There are two lines that begin with a single word and a full stop. Why do you think the writer does this?
7 What overall effect does the voice of the god have on you, the reader?

Words/phrases to explore (AO1 and AO2)

Bearing in mind what you've found in answering the questions in Activity 1, what can you say about the last line in the poem? Try to suggest more than one point.

Comparing with other poems

1 **Comparing ideas and themes**
   Compare the central characters in 'The River God' and 'Medusa'.
2 **Comparing writers' devices**
   Compare the ways the power of the characters in 'The River God' and 'Medusa' are created.

▶ **Poem Glossary**

weir a low dam built across a river, which causes water to flow quickly downstream

GradeStudio

Sample answer Ⓑ

To achieve a B on this AO1 descriptor, you need to make a **considered response**. To do this, you need to think about more than one thing. The following extract from a sample answer would hit the grade B requirement:

Activity 1, question 2
In some ways the god seems to be kind, as he blesses the fish and seems to like people swimming, and having fun. It is very sinister fun, though, as it includes a deliberate drowning and imprisonment of the body.

The Hunchback in the Park

by Dylan Thomas

Read the poem in your AQA Anthology,
then complete the activities below.

Initial responses

1 Which lines in the first **stanza** make the hunchback seem more like part of nature than human? How do they do this?

2 Now look carefully through the rest of the poem for more examples of words and phrases which make him seem part of nature.

3 The writer also shows him as being like an animal. Where does he do this?

4 'On out of sound' at the end of the third stanza seems to be from the hunchback's perspective – he can't hear them any more.
Some of the poem seems to be just described, perhaps by the 'I' in the second stanza, but not all of it.
  a Which other parts seem to be from the hunchback's point of view?
  b Which parts seem to be from the boys' point of view?

5 In the fourth stanza the trees are described as a 'loud zoo'. Why? Think of as many reasons as you can. Try seeing the phrase from all the points of view in the poem.

6 In the fifth stanza, how does the writer get inside the minds of the boys?

7 In the sixth stanza, how does the writer get inside the mind of the hunchback? What does this stanza show about him?

8 **a** In the last stanza, what things have followed the hunchback out of the park? How?
  b Now think about the word 'unmade'. How has the park been 'unmade'?

Words/phrases to explore (AO1)

Now you've explored the poem, think again about the 'I' in the second stanza.
a Who do you think he is, and how old is he?
b What do you think his response is to the hunchback, and to the boys? When you've decided this, think very carefully about how you reached your opinion from the details of the poem.

Comparing with other poems

1 Comparing ideas and themes
Compare the central characters of 'The Clown Punk' and 'The Hunchback in the Park'.

2 Comparing writers' devices
Compare the ways the central characters are created in 'The Clown Punk' and 'The Hunchback in the Park'.

GradeStudio

Sample answer (A)

To achieve an A on this AO1 descriptor, you need to show **exploratory response to text**. To do this, you need to think carefully about how you might respond to the characters and events in the poem. The following extract from a sample answer would hit the grade A requirement.

> In some ways, the boys are clearly behaving badly towards the hunchback, mocking this pathetic figure, but his longing for a woman figure '... straight as a young elm' might make the reader feel differently about him. The boys are just shown as young boys, after all, who are innocent, as shown by...

The Ruined Maid

by Thomas Hardy

Read the poem in your AQA Anthology, then complete the activities below.

Initial responses

1 Who are the two **speakers** in the poem, do you think, and what are the differences between them?
2 What does the first speaker admire about the second? If you look for all the individual things you might come to a general view.
3 In the fourth **stanza** the first speaker says about Melia 'your little gloves fit as on any la-dy!' Why might she be surprised by this? What do you think she means by 'la-dy' here, and how could it be seen as ironic?
4 How is the speech of the two characters different, and what does it show about them? Think about **tone** as well as words.
5 The **rhyme scheme** is very simple. Why do you think Hardy has chosen to do this?
6 In each stanza except the last, the first speaker has the third line and Melia the fourth. How does the **rhyme** add to the effect of conversation?
7 The last stanza is different, as Melia has the last two lines to herself. Why do you think Hardy has chosen to do this?

Words/phrases to explore (AO1 and AO2)

'You ain't ruined' says Melia at the end of the poem.
1 To what extent is each of the characters 'ruined'?
2 Think about the title. Which of the two women does this apply to most? In what sense is she 'ruined'?

Comparing with other poems

1 **Comparing ideas and themes**
   Compare the ways in which women are presented in 'The Ruined Maid' and 'Les Grands Seigneurs'.
2 **Comparing writers' devices**
   Compare the ways in which **dialect** is used in 'The Ruined Maid' and 'Singh Song'.

▶ Poem Glossary

spudding up docks digging up weeds

barton barn

megrims migraine

GradeStudio

Sample answer (B)

To achieve a B on this AO2 descriptor, you need to show **thoughtful consideration of ideas/themes**. To do this, you need to think of more than one idea about the poem. The following extract from a sample answer would hit the grade B requirement.

> Activity 1, question 2
> Melia is admired by her country friend as she has escaped a miserable existence by being 'ruined'. The irony is obvious, but there are two truths here: Melia may not really be a 'lady', but her friend is still enslaved.

Casehistory:
Alison (head injury)

by U.A. Fanthorpe

Read the poem in your AQA Anthology,
then complete the activities below.

▶ **Poem Glossary**

Degas dancer   Degas was a
French impressionist artist. Many of his
portraits were of ballet dancers

autocratic   regal, queenly

Initial responses

Activity 1

1   The poem opens with (*She looks at her photograph*). When you have
read the whole poem, what effect do you think this has on the reader?

2   The first **stanza** reads a bit like a puzzle.
   a   When the reader has worked it out, why does she not know
herself?
   b   Reading it again, what is the effect of the last word of the stanza?

3   Look at the sentence beginning 'Enmeshed'. Which words that
she uses about herself are chosen to deliberately contrast with the
younger self, do you think?

4   Why do you think the writer chooses to isolate the word 'Hardly' as
she does, after a stanza break and before a full stop?

5   The younger Alison did things that are beyond the older woman,
such as 'her A levels'. In stanzas 5 and 6, what did the younger
Alison do which the older woman can't?

6   Why do you think the writer uses the word 'her' three times in stanza 8?

7   Why do you think the writer places 'A bright girl she was' on a
separate line at the end of the poem, after the repetition of 'her'
before it?

Words/phrases to explore (AO1 and AO2)

Activity 2

1   What is the effect of the last line, repeated from earlier in the poem?

2   What attitude does the older Alison seem to have? Try to think of at
least two answers to this.

Comparing with other poems

Activity 3

1   **Comparing ideas and themes**
Compare the central characters in 'Casehistory: Alison' and 'Medusa'.

2   **Comparing writers' devices**
Compare the effects of the endings of 'Casehistory: Alison' and
'Medusa'.

GradeStudio

Sample answer Ⓐ

To achieve an A on this AO2
descriptor, you need to show
**analysis of writers' uses of
language and/or structure and/or
form and their effect on readers**.
To do this, you carefully unpick
how a device works. The following
extract from a sample answer
would hit the grade A requirement.

Activity 1, question 4
'Hardly' is isolated by
the stanza break and
the following full stop,
so that the reader
cannot miss its effect.
Following the flow of the
lines about the dancer's
movement, 'hardly'
– meaning the older
woman can hardly climb
the stairs – doubles the
effect of the clumsy 'lug'
in the previous line.

GradeStudio

Sample answer A*

To achieve an A* on this AO2 descriptor, you need to show **evaluation of writers' uses of language and/or structure and/or form and their effect on readers**. To do this, you carefully unpick how a device works, and show its final effect on you as the student has done in the answer below.

Activity I, question 7

The structure of most of the stanzas follows the same pattern: the stanza begins with something positive about the speaker's father, only to be brought down by a graphic and often gruesome reminder of the physical reality of his death, such as the 'maggots in his eyes'. The last stanza, however, is different in two ways: the thought is religious, not physical, and is despondent from the first line. The writer seems bitter about the death, not just accepting. What has decayed along with the body is his faith, it seems.

On a Portrait of a Deaf Man

by John Betjeman

Read the poem in your AQA Anthology, then complete the activities below.

Initial responses
Activity 1

1   The adjective 'kind' in the first line starts to establish the character of the **speaker's** father. What other words can you find in the poem which add to the picture?
2   List all the activities that the 'deaf man' used to like. What do these add to the impression you get of his character?
3   How does the writer play with the idea of eating in a gruesome way in the second **stanza**?
4   The fourth stanza is also deliberately gruesome. How does the writer use **rhyme** to add to the effect?
5   Now look at the seventh stanza. Like stanzas 2 and 4, there is a gruesome idea here about the corpse.
    a   How are these stanzas structured in a similar way?
    b   How does the writer use rhyme to add to the effect?
6   There's another rhyme in the last stanza which works in a similar way. What two things does the rhyme simultaneously connect and contrast?
7   'I only see decay.' How does the whole poem lead up to this last word?

Words/phrases to explore (AO1)
Activity 2

John Betjeman was in many ways a religious man. What do you think the last sentence of the poem says about his belief, and about his relationship with his father?

Comparing with other poems
Activity 3

1   **Ideas/themes to compare**
    Compare the feelings of the speakers in 'On a Portrait of a Deaf Man' and 'Brendon Gallacher'.
2   **Writer's devices to compare**
    Compare the effects of the endings of 'On a Portrait of a Deaf Man' and 'Ozymandias'.

Looking at the poems individually: what have you learned?

My learning ▶

In this section you will:
- think about which poems interested you most and why.

Complete Activities 1 and 2 below. As you do, think about which poems and which features of poems were most interesting to you. If you're working with someone else, you could learn from each other, or consider what differences in choices might reveal about you as readers.

Note that the words in bold in the tasks below refer to the key words in the Assessment Objectives.

Assessment Objective 1 (AO1)

Activity 1

1 Which of these poems did you **respond** to most strongly? You may have liked it, or disliked it, or found it the most interesting, or horrible. You may have a number of things to say about it.

2 Which poems did you find it easiest to offer an **interpretation** about? In other words, you had a view about a poem's meaning and could argue from the text and **select detail** to support your view. For instance, you might have found it easy to argue that the Duke in 'My Last Duchess' is a cold killer.

Suggesting more than one interpretation of a poem, or parts of a poem, gives you opportunities to score more marks. For instance, there are several ways in which you could respond to the main characters in 'Singh Song'.

Assessment Objective 2 (AO2)

Activity 2

1 Which features of **language**, **structure** or **form** did you understand best? The most promising ones to write about in the exam will be the ones where you have most to say. For instance, you might have found several things to say about:
- the effect of the metaphors for men in 'Les Grands Seigneurs' (language)
- the placing of 'Nothing beside remains' in 'Ozymandias' (structure)
- the effects of the rhyme at the end of 'The Clown Punk' (form).

When answering this question, it would be best if you chose your own examples rather than using the ones above!

2 What **ideas** did you identify in the poems? Again, the best answers will probably identify several ideas in a poem, or several aspects of one idea. For instance, you might have identified or explored a variety of attitudes expressed in 'Medusa', or a number of aspects of the importance of history in 'Checking Out Me History'.

My learning ▶

In this section you will learn how to:
- compare poems and address the Assessment Objectives
- develop writing skills and practise exam-style questions.

Comparing the 'Character and voice' poems

Assessment Objective 3 is broken into two parts:

▶ comparing ideas and themes in the poems, with detail

▶ comparing the ways writers use language or structure or form, with detail.

In responding to the exam question, you will need to address both these parts.

Comparing ideas and themes

Read the poems 'Les Grands Seigneurs' and 'Medusa', then complete the activities below.

Assessment Objective:

The Assessment Objective you will be focusing on in this part of the chapter is:

A03 make comparisons and explain links between texts, evaluating writers' different ways of expressing meaning and achieving effects.

Activity 1

Focusing on ideas and themes in the two poems, list as many similarities and differences as you can, for example: both the **speakers** are women; both women resent men; Medusa is aggressive while the woman in 'Les Grands Seigneurs' seems passive.

Activity 2

Using your list of similarities and differences from Activity 1, decide how different each of the poems are for each point you made. For example, both the speakers seem resentful towards men but are they equally resentful? What does each one resent?

Use quotations or refer to specific parts of the poem to support what you think.

GradeStudio

Sample answer **B**

To achieve a B on this AO3 descriptor, you need to make a **developed comparison in terms of ideas or themes**. The following extract from a sample answer would hit the grade B requirement.

The women's relationships with men seem to have changed immediately after marriage. In Medusa's case the change begins with 'a suspicion, a doubt, a jealousy' which then 'grew in my mind' suggesting a slow change whereas, in 'Les Grands Seigneurs', the change is instant, occurring 'overnight'. Medusa's change is far more dramatic, though: she physically changes (we don't know whether this happens in 'Les Grands Seigneurs'), and the man comes with 'a sword for a tongue', prepared for violence. The man in 'Les Grands Seigneurs', on the other hand, seems to be in control, clicking his fingers, and the woman seems passive.

Find a detail from each poem that you could compare. For example:

> I was their queen. I sat enthroned before them,
> Out of reach. We played at courtly love

(Les Grands Seigneurs)

> Wasn't I beautiful?
> Wasn't I fragrant and young?

(Medusa)

Write two or three paragraphs exploring all the similarities and differences you can find, asking yourself:

- How do the women see themselves?
- What is implied in each poem about the men's attitude to the women? How is each attitude implied?
- Is anything implied about the women's feelings now?
- How does each detail fit into the poem as a whole?

Comparing writers' methods

Now you need to think about the similarities and differences in terms of the methods the writers use, and why they use them. For example:

▶ both poems have short last lines, but they create different effects

▶ both refer to animals, but in 'Les Grands Seigneurs' animals are used as metaphors for men, whereas in 'Medusa' they are literal.

These are fairly simple links, though, rather than comparisons which explore or analyse. Better marks can usually be achieved by taking two details or quotations which have some similarity and exploring them.

Look at:

> The best and worst
> of times were men: the peacocks and the cockatoos,
> the nightingales, the strutting pink flamingos.

(Les Grands Seigneurs)

> And here you come
> with a shield for a heart
> and a sword for a tongue

(Medusa)

Explore the similarities and differences between these details.

1 How are the descriptions of men introduced?
2 What do the **metaphors** tell us about the **speaker's** attitude to men?
3 Think about the **rhythms** of the lines. What do the rhythms stress?

You should have found lots to say to form the basis of a detailed comparison. Choosing details about which you have plenty to say is a key skill.

GradeStudio

Sample answer A*

To achieve an A* on this AO3 descriptor, you need to make an **evaluative comparison of ideas and/or meanings and/ or techniques**. In the following extract both techniques and ideas are compared. The best answers will always do this.

Men are described more favourably by the woman in 'Les Grands Seigneurs' as she compares them to birds which are all beautiful in their own way. In 'Medusa', the man is described as simultaneously defensive and aggressive, with his 'shield' and 'sword'. That said, the men in 'Les Grands Seigneurs' do not get away unscathed: a 'peacock' is a metaphor for vanity, and perhaps arrogance, and 'cockatoos' manages to suggest both sexuality and silliness. This description comes early in the poem though: by the end of the poem men, in the form of the speaker's husband, are revealed as sexist and domineering. In 'Medusa' the man is described unfavourably from the start and by the end his 'heart' and 'tongue' are transformed to weapons. The man in 'Les Grands Seigneurs' seems to be getting his own way, but the man in 'Medusa' has a less certain fate.

Putting it all together

To practise the skills you've been working on in these comparison activities, here are two more activities on a different pair of poems: 'My Last Duchess' and 'The River God'.

1 What ideas and themes can you find in the poems which are similar? For example, both **speakers** are powerful. You might like to consider what attitudes to other people they have in common. List as many similarities as you can.

2 When you've established some similarities, think about what differences there are between the two poems, in terms of feelings and attitudes. List as many differences as you can.

3 Now you have a list of similarities and differences between the two speakers, you can consider how similar they are, or how different. For instance, they both seem to have caused a death, but what are the differences in their feelings towards their victims? How different are they really?

   For each similarity or difference, decide how similar or different the poems are. Include some detail or evidence to support each point.

4 Find a detail from each poem that you could compare directly, for example:

> that pictured countenance,
> The depth and passion of its earnest glance

(My Last Duchess)

> what a beautiful white face lies there
> Waiting for me to smoothe and wash away the fear
> She looks at me with.

(The River God)

If you chose these details to compare, the simple link between the two poems is that they both describe the victim's faces. However, to reach the grades you are aiming for, you need to explore all the similarities and differences you can find between the details. So here you would need to consider:

• What does each description say about the woman?
• What sort of feelings are evident here, from the victim and the speaker?
• How does each detail fit into the poems as a whole in what they reveal about the speaker?

Once you have chosen your two details, write two paragraphs comparing them.

GradeStudio

Sample answer A

To achieve an A on this AO3 descriptor, you need to make an **analytical comparison of ideas and/or meanings**. The following extract from a sample answer to question 3 in Activity 5 would hit the grade A requirement.

> Both speakers seem to admire the women they have killed, but to different degrees. The river god still seems to value her beauty: the word 'beautiful' is used three times close together, and her head is 'golden'. The Duke does see the 'depth and passion' in the Duchess' face, but is more concerned with his own importance: 'my favour at her breast'. The god still wants to treasure her, in his perverse way, as he wants to 'smoothe' her face. The Duke only treasures the dowry from his next victim.

Comparing writers' methods and purposes

Activity 6

Compare the ways in which the two writers finish the poems in the last three lines of each, exploring similarities and differences.

You should think about:
- how the two **speakers**' natures are revealed through their attitudes.
- how far each ending appears to be about the speaker himself, and how this is conveyed.
- which ending is directly about the victim, and which is indirect. With the latter, how might the reader be drawn into thinking about the victim?
- how the last line of each emphasises their characters.

GradeStudio

Sample answer B

To achieve a B on this AO3 descriptor, you need to make a **developed comparison of ideas and/or meanings and/or techniques**. The following extract from a sample answer would hit the grade B requirement.

> The god's exclamations seem to make him a much more enthusiastic, joyful figure: the zippy, funny rhythm of 'Hi yih, yippity-yap, merrily I flow' contrasts strongly with 'I choose/ Never to stoop', with the heavy stress on 'Never'. The god can be just as stern, though. The last words of the poem are 'I will not forgive her.' The strong, direct statement of will could have come from the Duke.

My learning ▶

In this section you will learn how to:
- structure a response in the exam
- use the skills you have learned to perform successfully.

Writing in the exam

Writing your response – planning and structuring

In the exam you have to show the skills that you practised in the activities on the previous pages, but how should you structure your writing to get the best marks you can? Your process with any exam question should be: Read, Think, Write, Edit.

Read

Read the questions – what exactly are you being asked to do? The questions should remind you about the Assessment Objectives. There will be a choice of two questions, so you need to make a choice quickly. Each question will ask you to compare a named poem with an unnamed poem, so your choice might be based on the poem that is named, or on what each question is asking you to do.

Think

This is the planning stage. The first word of the exam task is likely to be 'compare'. One of the descriptors in the mark band for a grade B is 'sustained and developed comparison'. This suggests that a wise course of action would be to build your response around a comparison of the two poems.

This doesn't mean that everything you write should be comparative. Rather, you should establish a comparative framework such as the one on page 28 before you write. Within that, you need to jot down quickly some of the ideas from the poems, and perhaps one or two details that you're planning to use – you should choose things that you can write quite a lot about.

The thinking is more important than the writing here. The whole process might take 5 minutes, perhaps (certainly not less than 2 minutes). You only have 45 minutes for the whole task. Don't start writing straight away, think about the question carefully first!

Assessment Objectives:

AO1 respond to texts critically and imaginatively; select and evaluate relevant textual detail to illustrate and support interpretations.

AO2 explain how language, structure and form contribute to writers' presentation of ideas, themes and settings.

AO3 make comparisons and explain links between texts, evaluating writers' different ways of expressing meaning and achieving effects.

Write

When you write, what you are going to show is:

▶ what you think about the poems

▶ why they are written in the ways that they are

▶ what happens when you compare the poems, or parts of them.

In other words, these are the things the Assessment Objectives focus on. The last phrase, 'or parts of them', is important. No question will ask you to write down everything you know about the poems; you have to select from what you know to think and write about the poems in answer to this question, in the ways that you've practised as you've worked through this section.

Edit

If you have any time left, you should look for ways to improve your answer. Don't look for spelling or punctuation errors: these don't carry marks here. Could you quickly add another possible meaning of a word or phrase that you've written about? Is there another idea about the effect of a writer's choice of language? Additions of this kind might gain you an extra mark.

Putting it into practice

Let's take a typical examination question:

Compare (AO3) the ways the writers present (AO2) a damaged character in 'Casehistory: Alison' and one other poem from 'Character and voice' (AO1).

Let's suppose that you chose 'On a Portrait of a Deaf Man' as a good poem to compare with 'Casehistory: Alison' – they are both first person narratives about a damaged person, but they describe different types of damage from different perspectives.   First, jot down a few ideas from the poems that you're going to use when you write. For example:

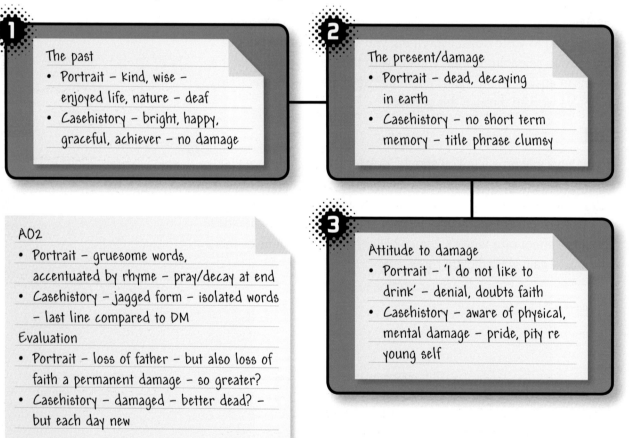

1

The past
- Portrait – kind, wise – enjoyed life, nature – deaf
- Casehistory – bright, happy, graceful, achiever – no damage

2

The present/damage
- Portrait – dead, decaying in earth
- Casehistory – no short term memory – title phrase clumsy

AO2
- Portrait – gruesome words, accentuated by rhyme – pray/decay at end
- Casehistory – jagged form – isolated words – last line compared to DM

Evaluation
- Portrait – loss of father – but also loss of faith a permanent damage – so greater?
- Casehistory – damaged – better dead? – but each day new

3

Attitude to damage
- Portrait – 'I do not like to drink' – denial, doubts faith
- Casehistory – aware of physical, mental damage – pride, pity re young self

In the notes above, the student has identified three areas to discuss in relation to damaged characters and jotted down some detail to use. They have made some notes on AO2 and jotted down a few ideas for evaluation. Of course, there are many more ideas that could be included, but the task is not to try to offer an exhaustive account – you are just showing off your thinking and writing skills, so three areas to focus on is plenty.

After thinking of three ideas, the student decided on the order they should go in (indicated by the numbers). Finally, they thought about how they were going to address AO2. Here, it would be good to contrast the gruesome words in 'On a Portrait of a Deaf Man' and the isolated words in 'Casehistory: Alison'.

Read the extracts from these sample student answers, together with the question below and the examiner comments. You could then try the sample exam question at the end.

Compare the ways the writers present a damaged character in 'Casehistory: Alison' and one other poem from 'Character and voice'.

Openings

 **grade answer**

Student A

The characters in both poems have a happy past, and seem to be admired. The father in 'Deaf Man' was 'kind' and 'wise' and seems to have enjoyed life, including such things as 'potatoes in their skins' and 'Cornish air'. Similarly, 'smiles' are mentioned three times in describing the younger Alison, and she is admired for her 'delicate ankles' and 'poise', her achievements, and being 'bright'. The father, though, is already mildly damaged: he is deaf, and he seems to have a dread of death shown by his reaction to Highgate cemetery. There is no hint of damage in the young Alison: even when she grieves for her father, she smiles.

Examiner comment

Student A's response is already a **developed comparison in terms of ideas**, with **thoughtful selection of material for comparison** and has already achieved a B.

A **grade answer**

Student B

It is difficult to say which of these characters is more damaged. In both poems, the speaker idealises the character's past life. These characters enjoyed life: 'liked' is used about five different things in relation to the father, and there are four mentions of Alison smiling, even in adversity. They have admirable skills, too: the father knows the name of every bird and can paint, and Alison is a 'bright' girl with A levels. Like the father, she is wise despite her tender years: she has 'digested mourning'.

Examiner comment

Student B's response is stronger in terms of comparison, as it becomes **analytical** in grouping the characters' qualities, for which they would achieve an A. With the first sentence, Student B also lays the groundwork for an evaluation of damage later in the response.

Examiner comment

Both these openings get straight on with the task. They avoid using 'In this essay I am going to write about… ', which is a waste of time.

GradeStudio

A paragraph on Assessment Objective 1 **AO1**

B grade answer

Student A

The attitudes of the speakers to the damage are similar in some ways. Both seem proud: the pride in the father is clear not only in the listing of his skills and his enjoyment of life, but also directly through words like 'kind' and 'wise', and the gentle education of his son. The older Alison is direct about pride itself: she is 'proud' of this younger self and 'asserts' her achievements. Her pride seems a little qualified, though: there seems to be a hint of jealousy because she cannot 'get over' her father's death, because she cannot consistently remember that it happened, and perhaps because of her 'autocratic knee'.

Examiner comment

Student A's response shows **considered/qualified response to text** and **details linked to interpretation**, both in the 19–24 mark band (equivalent to a Grade B).

A* grade answer

Student B

The attitudes to damage are quite different, because of the identity and nature of the speakers. It is true that both seem proud: the pride in the father is clear not only in the listing of his skills and his enjoyment of life, but also directly through words like 'kind' and 'wise', and the gentle education of his son. The older Alison is direct about pride itself: she is 'proud' of this younger self and 'asserts' her achievements. Her pride seems a little qualified, though: there seems to be a hint of jealousy because she cannot 'get over' her father's death, because she cannot consistently remember that it happened, and perhaps because of her 'autocratic knee'. It is the issue of faith that divides them most. The older Alison's mind would like to achieve the younger self's capacity for 'lack of faith', but cannot. The son in 'Portrait of a Deaf Man', though, thinks about his father in a clear, ordered way, and his conclusion about faith is completely clear at the end of the poem: his faith existed, and has been lost.

Examiner comment

Student B's response has much of the same material, but is centred around an idea, and deals more with AO3 as well. The two 19–24 AO3 descriptors are hit, and there is some **exploration of ideas** (25–30) and **evaluation** (31–36) about faith, too.

A paragraph on Assessment Objective 2 AO2

B grade answer

Student A

Both of the poems end dramatically. 'A bright girl she was' repeats the third line of the poem, creating an echo for the reader, and it is the only single line in the poem. Isolating it like this makes it feel like an epitaph. 'Portrait of a Deaf Man' feels like an epitaph throughout, but the repetition at the end is one that has been established right through the poem, as rhyme. The end is dramatic because 'pray' rhymes with 'decay', and connecting the two shows the speaker's loss of faith, and the reason for it.

Examiner comment

Student A finds two things to say about the effect of the last line of 'Casehistory: Alison', hitting **appreciation of writer's use of language** in the 19–24 mark band (equivalent to a grade B).

A* grade answer

Student B

The endings of both poems complete the patterns in the writing. 'A bright girl she was' echoes the third line, giving a sense of completion, but placing this as a single line completes and perfects a pattern of jagged thought, where syntax is sometimes strange, and 'Hardly' can appear as an isolated first word of a stanza. The girl's mind is jagged, and the writing matches it. A quite different pattern is completed in 'Portrait'. Each stanza apart from the fifth has moved from negative to positive, and four of them have emphasised the state of the body in the earth – 'shroud', 'clay', 'maggots', and 'finger-ends', with their deliberately gruesome images. This is completed with the summarising word 'decay'. This is a crushing ending, as it is a new development of thought – the rhyme with 'pray' underlines the decay of faith. This is a development which Alison is incapable of making.

Examiner comment

Student B's response is **analytical** about language and form, and shows **close analysis** of the detail of 'decay' and **evaluation** of the effect of this on the reader, so showing 25–30 and 31–36 (A and A*) qualities.

You are now ready to tackle an exam question. Here's one to try:

Compare how characters in difficulties are presented in 'The Clown Punk' and one other poem from 'Character and voice'.

When you've written your answer you could mark it, or get a partner to mark it, using the mark scheme on page 134.

My learning ▶

In this section you will learn how to:
- become familiar with the poems as a whole
- start to make links between the poems.

Getting to know the poems

The poems

The Blackbird of Glanmore
Seamus Heaney

A Vision
Simon Armitage

The Moment
Margaret Atwood

Cold Knap Lake
Gillian Clarke

Price We Pay for the Sun
Grace Nichols

Neighbours
Gillian Clarke

Crossing the Loch
Kathleen Jamie

Hard Water
Jean Sprackland

London
William Blake

The Prelude (extract)
William Wordsworth

The Wild Swans at Coole
W.B. Yeats

Spellbound
Emily Brontë

Below the Green Corrie
Norman McCaig

Storm in the Black Forest
D.H. Lawrence

Wind
Ted Hughes

Assessment Objectives:

A01 respond to texts critically and imaginatively; select and evaluate relevant textual detail to illustrate and support interpretations.

A02 explain how language, structure and form contribute to writers' presentation of ideas, themes and settings.

A03 make comparisons and explain links between texts, evaluating writers' different ways of expressing meaning and achieving effects.

Introduction

The poems in this chapter are centred around place, and the relationship between places and people. All the poems are in your AQA Anthology.

In this chapter you will be:

▶ looking at the individual poems

▶ comparing the poems

▶ learning how to approach exam questions.

As a result of this preparation you will be developing your writing skills in order to hit the Assessment Objectives. See page v for more information about what the Assessment Objectives mean. In the exam you will have to compare two poems from this chapter.

Getting started

The first thing to do is to start to familiarise yourself with the 'Place' poems. You can do the following activities by yourself, or in a group.

Read all the 'Place' poems in your AQA Anthology, quickly. Just notice what they seem to be about – don't worry about trying to make sense of every line.

Now find as many links as you can between some of the poems. You will need a large piece of paper with some headings on. Below is a list of ways you could look at the poems. You could use some of these to form your headings, though you could think of some of your own as well.

Ways to look at the poems	Tips on what to watch out for
What the poems are about	All the poems are about places, but there are very different attitudes to place. Which poems seem to have similar attitudes? Which have similar **tones**? Think about whether the poems seem reflective, happy, melancholy, or something else.
Beginnings/endings	Any similarities? Which poems end with a definite statement, for instance? Which endings seem to summarise the message or the mood of the poems?
Length	You might notice some distinct similarities or differences. Include the number and length of **stanzas**, if there are any.
Rhyme	You need to look a little more carefully now. Is there a regular **rhyme scheme**? Does it change? Be careful – some poems that don't seem to rhyme often use a lot of **half-rhyme** or **echoes**, like 'Cold Knap Lake', which has one **rhyming couplet** at the end. If you were working on this poem, you'd need to consider why the writer does this. 'London' rhymes all the way through, though – how does this add to the feeling Blake is creating?
Rhythm	Are there any poems with a strong **rhythm**, such as 'The Wild Swans at Coole'? Are any of the others similar to this?
Language	Some of these poems have striking **imagery**, such as 'Below the Green Corrie' and 'The Moment'. See if there are any similarities. Both 'Cold Knap Lake' and 'The Wild Swans at Coole' make use of swans, but differently – how? There's a lot of **personification**, too – look for it.
Imagery	Some poems are rich in **imagery** such as **metaphors** and **similes**, whereas others might seem quite plain. Make a note of some obvious similarities and differences.

Now that you have found a lot of links, try displaying your findings in a different way, on a sheet of A3 paper. Working on your own, in a pair or in a group, you could try any of the following ways.

1 Spread the titles out on the sheet and draw links between them, labelling each one.

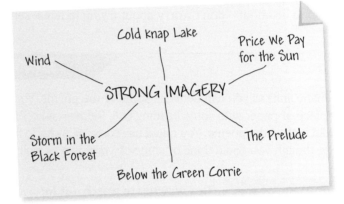

2 Draw a picture or symbol for each idea (such as death or nature) that appears in more than one poem, and group the poems around each – a poem can appear in more than one group.

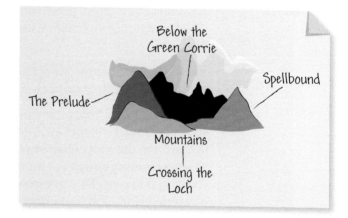

3 Draw a picture, or pictures, for each poem on the sheet, and link similar ones with arrows.

In these activities you have started to tackle all three Assessment Objectives. Now you will be focusing on AO1 and AO2 as you look at the poems individually (pages 35–51). You will return to AO3 when you compare the poems (pages 52–56). Finally, you will look at how to turn your knowledge and skills into successful exam answers, before you attempt one yourself (pages 57–61).

Looking at the poems individually

My learning ▶

In this section you will learn how to:
- develop your responses to the poems
- relate the Assessment Objectives to the poems.

This section of the chapter, pages 35–51, is designed to lead you through an exploration of each individual poem. Throughout, you will find examples of student responses at different levels.

In the exam you will have to write about the poems individually as well as comparing them.

In the exam you have to compare two poems; one named poem and one unnamed poem, which means you can choose the second one. On the Higher Tier paper the following will not be named poems: 'A Vision', 'Price We Pay for the Sun', 'Spellbound'. Of course, you could choose any of these poems to compare with the named one.

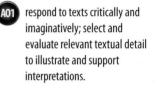

Assessment Objectives:

The Assessment Objectives you will be focusing on in this part of the chapter are:

AO1 respond to texts critically and imaginatively; select and evaluate relevant textual detail to illustrate and support interpretations.

AO2 explain how language, structure and form contribute to writers' presentation of ideas, themes and settings.

The Blackbird of Glanmore

by Seamus Heaney

Read the poem in your AQA Anthology, then complete the activities below.

Initial responses

Activity 1

1   In the poem the **speaker** reflects on his life. Look at the two lines beginning 'I park'. How does Heaney convey a sense of reflection here by the words, the punctuation and the shape of the lines?
2   Look at the three lines beginning 'And I think of one gone to him'.
    a   Who has the brother gone to?
    b   How was he like the blackbird?
    c   Why do you think Heaney describes the brother as 'Haunter-son'?
3   What do the neighbour's words suggest about the bird? Think about the effect of the tale in the poem as a whole – this is not just a bird.
4   Find the words that break the silence and reflection. How does Heaney use the sound of words to make the moment sharp?
5   In the three lines beginning 'I've a bird's eye view', Heaney imagines the blackbird's perspective of him, but it is not just literal.
    a   How could he be 'a shadow' in his 'house of life'?
    b   What does this make the blackbird seem to be?
6   The last line 'In the ivy when I leave' is repeated from earlier in the poem, but this time as a line on its own.
    a   What is the effect of the gap between the last two lines, do you think?
    b   How is the blackbird made to seem a constant presence in the whole poem?

Words/phrases to explore (AO1 and AO2)

Activity 2

Now you have read the whole poem, think about the phrase 'I am absolute/For you.' What do you think Heaney accepts fully when he admires the blackbird?

Comparing with other poems

Activity 3

1   **Comparing ideas and themes**
    Compare the relationship between humans and nature in 'The Blackbird of Glanmore' and 'The Wild Swans at Coole'.
2   **Comparing writers' devices**
    Compare the ways in which the writers use **structure** in 'The Blackbird of Glanmore' and 'The Wild Swans at Coole'.

A Vision

by Simon Armitage

Read the poem in your AQA Anthology, then complete the activities below.

Initial responses

1 **a** What is the attitude to the plan of the future town in the poem as a whole?
   b How is that attitude shown in the first **stanza**?
2 What in the second stanza makes the 'vision' seem unreal?
3 **a** What in the second stanza suggests someone is playing?
   b Can you find a similar idea in the third stanza?
4 **a** Which word in the fourth stanza suggests that the town is very 'grand' for ordinary people?
   b Which other words in the poem suggest the same thing?
5 How does Armitage show in the last stanza that the 'vision' was unreal, and never happened? Think about the words he uses here which are different from the words in the rest of the poem, and his choice for the last word.

Words/phrases to explore (AO1 and AO2)

Now you have read the whole poem, look at the first line again. How exactly does this line set up the whole poem, both in what it says and the choices Armitage has made?

Comparing with other poems

1 **Comparing ideas and themes**
   Compare the views of society shown in 'A Vision' and 'London'.
2 **Comparing writers' devices**
   Compare how the writers of 'A Vision' and 'Wind' capture the mood of the poems in the opening lines.

▶ **Poem Glossary**

fuzzy-felt grass a piece of green material to look like grass on the model

Fuzzy-Felt a child's toy consisting of a flocked backing board and a number of felt shapes that can be used to create many different pictures

Grade**Studio**

Sample answer B

To achieve a B on this AO2 descriptor, you need to show **appreciation/consideration of writers' uses of language and/ or structure and/or form and their effects on readers.** The following extract from a sample answer would hit the grade B requirement.

Activity 2
The punctuation at the end of the first line emphasises the defeat of the vision: the comma and then the full stop both lift out the word 'once' and give it finality as the sentence and the line end.

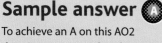

▶ Poem Glossary

fissure split

GradeStudio

Sample answer Ⓐ

To achieve an A on this AO2 descriptor, you need to show **analysis of writers' uses of language and/or form and/or structure and their effects on readers**. The following extract from a sample answer would hit the grade A requirement.

> **Activity 1, question 3**
>
> The gap between the first and second stanzas, emphasised by the comma after 'this', has two effects: it seems to act as a pause for reflection on people's achievement, but then becomes a moment to reflect on their arrogance.

The Moment

by Margaret Atwood

Read the poem in your AQA Anthology, then complete the activities below.

Initial responses

Activity 1

1 'A long voyage' could mean a sea voyage, but what else might it mean?
2 How does the progression of places work in lines 3 and 4? Try to imagine it.
3 Why do you think the writer places a gap between **stanzas** after the words 'I own this'?
4 In the first stanza there is a list of places, and in the second stanza there is a list of things that happen.
   a What direction does the list in the second stanza move in, compared to the first?
   b How does the writer make the things in the second stanza seem bigger and more active? Think about the number of words used, the language devices she uses, and the effects of the events she describes.
5 What is the first line of the last stanza a reply to?
6 What does the word 'proclaiming' suggest to you about humans' activities?
7 What does 'You never found us' suggest about humans' relationship with nature?

Words/phrases to explore (AO1 and AO2)

Activity 2

Bearing in mind what you have found in answering the questions in Activity 1:
1 What can you say about the last line?
2 What do you think 'the other way round' means?
3 How does the **structure** of the poem mirror 'the other way round'? Think about the voices that speak as well as the things you have already seen.

Comparing with other poems

Activity 3

1 **Comparing ideas and themes**
   Compare the relationship between humans and nature in 'The Moment' and 'Wind'.
2 **Comparing writers' devices**
   Compare the ways in which the writers of 'The Moment' and 'Wind' use **personification** to suggest the power of nature.

Cold Knap Lake
by Gillian Clarke

Read the poem in your AQA Anthology, then complete the activities below.

Initial responses

Activity 1

1   **a** What do you think is 'the water's long green silk'?
    b Why do you think the poet describes it like this?
    c Look for all the other colours in the poem, and decide what each one suggests.

2   The first three **stanzas** are written from the point of view of a child. How does the poet show that it is a child's viewpoint?

3   There is a full stop after 'the dread of it', and then a comma after 'breathed'. What effect do these two pauses have on the reader?

4   'Was I there?' comes after a gap, and is the shortest line in the poem.
    a Why do you think the poet makes these choices?
    b How does the time of the poem alter at this point?

5   The sentences in the fourth stanza are questions.
    a What is the **speaker** uncertain about?
    b Which words in the stanza suggest uncertainty, or things being lost?

6   There are some echoes and **half-rhymes** in the poem, but the only full **rhyme** in the poem is formed by the last two lines.
    a Why do you think the poet decided to do this?
    b What things is she joining together?

7   There is a lot of **alliteration** here, too, which ties things together – look for 'l'. 'Closing' suggests something happening now. What are we always losing, just like the speaker in the poem?

Words/phrases to explore (AO1 and AO2)

Activity 2

The last two lines seem almost like part of a nursery rhyme. What else in the poem seems to be like a children's story, and what seems very adult?

Comparing with other poems

Activity 3

1   **Comparing ideas and themes**
    Compare the effects of memory in 'Cold Knap Lake' and 'The Wild Swans at Coole'.

2   **Comparing writers' devices**
    Compare how Gillian Clarke shapes the endings of 'Cold Knap Lake' and 'Neighbours' to affect the reader.

GradeStudio

Sample answer (A*)

To achieve an A* on this AO2 descriptor, you need to show **evaluation of writers' uses of language and/or structure and/or form and their effects on readers**. The following extract from a sample answer would hit the grade A* requirement.

> **Activity 1, question 7**
> The 'l' alliteration ties together the 'lake' and the 'lost things', but they are under 'closing' water: the process of loss of memory is continual. The 'daughter' of the poor man is lost to the other daughter in the poem, not in death but in memory, which the rhyming couplet underlines dramatically.

Price We Pay for the Sun

by Grace Nichols

Read the poem in your AQA Anthology, then complete the activities below.

Initial responses

1 Who is the poem addressed to? What is your evidence for your view?
2 Why does Nichols repeat the word 'real'?
3 How does Nichols introduce the comparison between the island and its inhabitants in the first **stanza**?
4 What features of the island that are not like 'picture postcards' are mentioned in the second stanza?
5 How are these features compared to bad things happening to the **speaker's** family?
6 Why do you think Nichols describes her mother's cancer as 'sulph-furious'? (Remember that she is comparing the island's features to its inhabitants.)
7 Now look back to the end of the first stanza. More than 'stone' and 'foam', the islands 'split bone'. What do you think this means?
8 a What is contrasted with 'poverty' in the last three lines?
   b Do you think the last two words also form a contrast? Why?

GradeStudio

Sample answer B

To achieve a B on this AO1 descriptor, you need to show **details linked to interpretation**. The following extract from a sample answer would hit the grade B requirement.

> **Activity 1, question 4**
> Nichols shows clearly that the islands, although they are beautiful, contain the possibilities of pain: the volcanoes may be 'sleeping', but they are there, and the winds become 'salty hurricanes' – people suffer, like anywhere else.

Words/phrases to explore (AO1 and AO2)

Now that you have read the whole poem, look at the last three lines of the poem and the first three. What is Nichols saying about the islands overall?

Comparing with other poems

1 **Comparing ideas and themes**
   Compare how the reality of a place is shown in 'Price We Pay for the Sun' and 'Hard Water'.
2 **Comparing writers' devices**
   Compare how a place is made to seem unpleasant in 'Price We Pay for the Sun' and 'London'.

Neighbours

by Gillian Clarke

Read the poem in your AQA Anthology, then complete the activities below.

Initial responses

Activity 1

1 What signs are there in the first **stanza** that there is something wrong in nature?
2 Go through the poem and jot down all the other examples you can find of things being 'wrong'.
3 'A mouthful of bitter air' (fourth stanza). Why is the air described as 'bitter'? Try to think of more than one reason.
4 What does the 'box of sorrows' refer to, and why is it described like this?
5 Why is the rain described as a 'poisoned arrow'? Think about both words.
6 What exactly do you think the writer means by 'neighbourly' in the sixth stanza? Think about geographical and personal relationships. How else is the importance of this idea signalled?
7 How are 'the virus and the toxin' like a democracy?
8 Why are they looking for a bird 'with green in its voice'? Think of the various associations with the word 'green'.

Words/phrases to explore (AO1 and AO2)

Activity 2

Analyse the last three lines.
1 Why do you think the writer uses two other languages here?
2 What does the 'break of blue' imply? Think of as many reasons as you can.
3 Why do you think the lines are shorter here than in the rest of the poem? Look at the shape of the lines on the page.

Comparing with other poems

Activity 3

1 **Comparing ideas and themes**
   Compare the unpleasant aspects of nature shown in 'Neighbours' and 'Price We Pay for the Sun'.
2 **Comparing writers' devices**
   Compare the effects of the endings of 'Neighbours' and 'Cold Knap Lake'.

GradeStudio

Poem context

The **Chernobyl disaster** was a nuclear reactor accident in 1986 in Ukraine. It resulted in the release of radioactivity into the atmosphere over a wide area, which affected human beings, birds, animals and food production.

▶ Poem Glossary

caesium a dangerous element released into the atmosphere from the disaster

fjords narrow sea inlets on the Norwegian coast

gall poisonous bitter liquid

glasnost (Russian) open process of government (a word associated with the liberalisation of the Soviet Union in the late 1980s)

golau glas (Welsh) blue light

GradeStudio

Sample answer **B**

To achieve a B on this AO2 descriptor, you need to show **details linked to interpretation** as in the sample answer below.

> Activity 2, question 2
>
> The poem is full of poison – 'gall', 'bitter air', 'the poisoned arrow'. At the end, though, hope appears twice, in the 'green' of the bird's voice, with its suggestions of new life and Spring, and the 'break of blue' suggesting a clear rather than a poisoned sky.

▶ Poem Glossary

the loch a loch is a lake in Scotland; some Scottish sea lochs are used as bases for nuclear submarines

sickle-shaped shaped like a curved blade

phosphorescence natural phenomenon of glowing lights appearing in water at night

anklet an ornamental chain worn round the ankle

in the race in a strong current of water

GradeStudio

Sample answer Ⓐ

To achieve an A on this AO2 descriptor, you need to show **analysis of writers' uses of language and/or structure and/or form and their effects on readers**. To do this you need to examine a writer's choice carefully. The following extract from a sample answer would hit the grade A requirement.

> **Activity 2, question 1**
> The boat's movement in the water is captured in two ways at the beginning of the second stanza: the rhythm of 'splash, creak,' followed by the commas make brief pauses as the oars dip, and the rest of the line and the uninterrupted next line match the glide created. At the same time, the sounds of the dipping oars are created for the reader.

Crossing the Loch

by Kathleen Jamie

Read the poem in your AQA Anthology, then complete the activities below.

Initial responses
Activity 1

1 The first word of the poem is 'Remember'. Look through the rest of the poem and jot down all the words and phrases that remind the reader that this is a poem of memory – what is remembered and what is not.
2 At the end of the first **stanza**, how does the writer use the idea of a mouth to describe the start of the journey?
3 Look at the second stanza.
   a What dangers are mentioned or suggested in the stanza?
   b How does the writer use the senses of hearing and touch to capture the feelings of the people in the boat?
4 In the third stanza, how is the boat 'like a twittering nest'? Think about both words.
5 How is the boat like a 'small boat of saints'? Think of the effect of the phosphorescence.
6 Why is the bow wave like a 'magic dart', do you think?
7 How does the end of the poem bring the reader back to the beginning of the journey?

Words/phrases to explore (AO2)
Activity 2

'The oars' splash, creak, and the spill/of the loch reached long into the night'.
1 How exactly does the writer create the sensation of the boat's movement here? Listen to the **rhythm** of the lines, and work out how it is created.
2 What do you think the second line means?

Comparing with other poems
Activity 3

1 **Comparing ideas and themes**
   Compare the experiences of rowing at night in 'Crossing the Loch' and 'The Prelude'.
2 **Comparing writers' devices**
   Compare the ways in which the writers use light in 'Crossing the Loch' and 'Storm in the Black Forest'.

Hard Water

by Jean Sprackland

Read the poem in your AQA Anthology, then complete the activities below.

Initial responses

Activity 1

1 The first three lines are about a holiday experience. Why do you think there is a break after these lines?

2 'Hey up me duck' is a **dialect** expression that belongs to the **speaker's** home town. What else does the speaker like about her home town? Make a list.

3 What do you think the 'little fizz of anxiety' is? Think about the water and the speaker's state of mind.

4 'It couldn't lie.' What does the water tell the truth about? Look at the two lines that follow.

5 Look at the four lines beginning 'I let a different cleverness'.
   a The writer has 'book-learning', but what is the 'cleverness' of her home city?
   b How do these four lines use the idea of water?

6 Who do you think might have said 'too bloody deep for me', and why?

7 The writer is marked as 'belonging, regardless.' What does she belong to, do you think, and 'regardless' of what?

Words/phrases to explore (AO1 and AO2)

Activity 2

Remind yourself of the words 'Flat. Straight.'
1 What do these two words apply to? Think of more than one thing.
2 How does the way the words are written add to the effect?

Comparing with other poems

Activity 3

1 **Comparing ideas and themes**
   Compare the feelings of the speaker in 'Hard Water' and 'The Blackbird of Glanmore'.

2 **Comparing writers' devices**
   Compare the ways in which the writers use the senses in 'Hard Water' and 'Wind'.

GradeStudio

Sample answer Ⓐ

To achieve an A on this AO2 descriptor, you need to show **exploration of ideas/themes**. To do this you need to think carefully about the ideas in the poem. The following extract from a sample answer would hit the grade A requirement.

> **Activity 1, question 4**
> The poem is about identity, in the end. The water is 'honest', 'couldn't lie', and the speaker is defining the truth about herself. Despite the 'book-learning' which threatens to divorce her from her roots, and the excitement of other places, symbolised by the soft water in Wales, it is the 'true taste' of work and early mornings and the straight talking of this place which define her, she feels.

London

by William Blake

Read the poem in your AQA Anthology, then complete the activities below.

Initial responses

Activity 1

1 Look through the whole poem, and pick out all the words that suggest grief, danger, destruction or cruelty.
2 The word 'charter'd' is repeated in the first and second lines.
   a What is the effect of this, do you think?
   b Find the other repetitions in the poem, and decide what effects they have.
   c What is the overall effect of having so many repetitions, do you think?
3 What 'marks' do you think the **speaker** sees?
4 Look at the phrase 'mind-forg'd manacles'.
   a How are the people in the city tied?
   b How are their bonds 'mind-forg'd', do you think?
5 a What were working conditions like for early nineteenth-century chimney sweeps? (You might need to do some research, possibly on the Internet, to help you here.)
   b How do you interpret the line 'Every blackening church appals'?
6 In Blake's picture of London, everything that should be innocent or happy is not. Find three examples of this in the last few lines.

Poem Glossary

charter'd planned, mapped
hapless unfortunate
harlot a female prostitute
manacles handcuffs

GradeStudio

Sample answer Ⓐ

To achieve an A on this AO1 descriptor, you need to show **analytical use of detail to support interpretation**. The following extract from a sample answer would hit the grade A requirement.

> Activity 1, question 2
> Every detail Blake uses in his hellish vision is strengthened by the adjectives: the Harlot has to be 'youthful', the Infant 'new born', the Church 'black'ning', the Soldier 'hapless'. 'Charter'd' suggests there is no escape from these confines.

Words/phrases to explore (AO1 and AO2)
Activity 2

Say the poem aloud, noticing the steady **rhythm** and regular **rhyme**, as well as the repeated words and phrases. Now explain how this connects to Blake's views about London in the poem. Think particularly about the word 'every' – how is everything in the poem part of the same view of the city?

Comparing with other poems
Activity 3

1 **Comparing ideas and themes**
   Compare the visions of destruction in 'London' and 'Wind'.
2 **Comparing writers' devices**
   Compare how the writers of 'London' and 'Wind' use words that suggest danger and malice.

The Prelude (extract)

by William Wordsworth

Read the poem in your AQA Anthology, then complete the activities below.

Initial responses

Activity 1

1 When the boy starts to row, Wordsworth uses sound and sight to convey what happens.
  a How does Wordsworth prepare the reader for what happens later by the way he describes the echo of the oars?
  b How does he use what he sees to suggest the distance the boat travels?
2 Read the lines from 'But now' to 'like a swan' (lines 11–20). How does Wordsworth suggest the boy's enjoyment in the place and the activity in these lines?
3 Look at the lines from 'When, from behind' to 'Strode after me.' (lines 21–29). The mountains suddenly seem threatening. How does Wordsworth achieve this? Think about:
  a the ways the mountains are **personified** (made to seem living)
  b the actions, and where the words describing them are placed
  c the adjectives.
4 The boy's mood has changed from the opening. He has two responses to what happens. What is his immediate response, and what does he think about it later?
5 What do you think the boy means by 'huge and mighty forms, that do not live/Like living men'?

Words/phrases to explore (AO1 and AO2)

Activity 2

Now you have explored the movement of the extract, look back and find where Wordsworth uses a verb as the first word of a line. What effect do these words have at the time, and then on the pace of the piece as a whole?

Comparing with other poems

Activity 3

1 **Comparing ideas and themes**
  Compare how the countryside is presented in 'The Prelude' and 'Below the Green Corrie'.
2 **Comparing writers' devices**
  Compare the ways in which the writers of 'The Prelude' and 'Below the Green Corrie' present threatening experiences.

▶ **Poem Glossary**

(led by her) 'her' refers to Nature in the poem
elfin pinnace a small light boat
instinct infused, full of
covert hiding place

GradeStudio

Sample answer (A*)

To achieve an A* on this AO2 descriptor, you need to show **evaluation of writers' use of language and/or structure and/or form and their effects on readers**. The following extract from a sample answer would hit the grade A* requirement.

> **Activity 2**
> Wordsworth uses verbs at the beginning of lines to telling effect. Early in the incident 'pushed', combined with 'straight' in the previous line, gets the action quickly and simply under way, as the boy innocently sets out; but when the mountains appear, 'upreared' and then 'towered' escalate size and then threat, while 'strode' followed by 'after me' is simply terrifying for the boy. The reader can feel the extent of his panic even before it is verbalised with 'trembling'.

The Wild Swans at Coole

by W.B. Yeats

Read the poem in your AQA Anthology, then complete the activities below.

GradeStudio

Context

Swans are known to mate for life.

▶**Poem Glossary**

clamorous noisy

GradeStudio

Sample answer **B**

To achieve a B on this AO2 descriptor, you need to show **thoughtful consideration of ideas/themes**. The following extract from a sample answer would hit the grade B requirement.

> Activity 2
>
> The effects of nature on the speaker, in the shape of the swans, are several. Clearly he delights in the 'beautiful', 'brilliant creatures', and admires their apparent longevity and constancy; at the same time, though, this makes him reflect on the changes that have happened to him with age. 'Lighter' then suggests heavier now, and a 'sore heart': sore with age, perhaps, but maybe also lacking in the 'passion' and 'conquest' the swans still have.

Initial responses

Activity 1

1 'Under the October twilight' gives the time of day and the time of year. October is when the swans depart – but why else might these times be suitable for the poem?
2 The first **stanza** seems very still, and the second very active. How does Yeats achieve this? Think about the words he uses, and the effect of the short lines.
3 In the third stanza the **speaker's** heart is 'sore'.
   a Why, do you think?
   b What might have changed?
4 a In the fourth stanza, how do the swans seem unchanged?
   b How might the speaker have changed, unlike the swans?
5 Why does the speaker think of the swans as 'mysterious'?
6 Why does Yeats choose to end the poem with a question?

Words/phrases to explore (AO1 and AO2)

Activity 2

Now you have explored the poem, what is the effect of the swans on the speaker? Think about what he reveals about his mood, and how they are described, both in the way they look and the sounds associated with them.

Comparing with other poems

Activity 3

1 **Comparing ideas and themes**
   Compare the memories presented in 'Crossing the Loch' and 'The Wild Swans at Coole'.
2 **Comparing writers' devices**
   Compare the ways in which the writers of 'The Wild Swans at Coole' and 'Cold Knap Lake' use swans in the poems.

Spellbound

by Emily Brontë

Read the poem in your AQA Anthology, then complete the activities below.

▶ **Poem Glossary**

drear dreary, gloomy

Initial responses

Activity 1

1 Why is the spell the **speaker** seems to be under described as a 'tyrant' spell?
2 What is the effect of the repetition of 'cannot' at the end of the first **stanza**?
3 Which words in the second stanza make the conditions seem more threatening?
4 What do the first two lines of the last stanza say about the speaker's mental state, do you think?
5 Look at the last line of the poem. How has the speaker's determination strengthened from the first stanza?
6 Looking at the poem overall, how is the speaker's mental state conveyed? Look for repetitions of words and sounds in lines, between lines, and between stanzas.

Words/phrases to explore (AO1 and AO2)

Activity 2

Now you have explored the **tone** of the whole poem in Activity 1, think again about the line 'Wastes beyond wastes below'. How could this line reflect the whole poem, both in what it says and the way it is written?

Comparing with other poems

Activity 3

1 **Comparing ideas and themes**
   Compare the feelings of the speakers in 'Spellbound' and 'The Prelude'.
2 **Comparing writers' devices**
   Compare how the writers of 'Spellbound' and 'Storm in the Black Forest' use repetitions.

GradeStudio

Sample answer Ⓑ

To achieve a B on this AO1 descriptor, you need to show **considered/qualified response to text**. The following extract from a sample answer would hit the grade B requirement.

Activity 1, question 5

The speaker in the poem seems terrified by the conditions, as shown by adjectives such as 'wild' and 'giant', so that she is unable to move; but 'I will not' in the last line suggests something else is going on in her mind beyond mere terror.

Below the Green Corrie

by Norman McCaig

Read the poem in your AQA Anthology, then complete the activities below.

Initial responses

Activity 1

1 The mountains are personified (made to seem like living things) right through the poem, beginning with 'like bandits'. Find all the other examples of **personification** in the poem.
2 How does the writer convey a sense of threat in the first **stanza**? Think about the words and the ideas.
3   **a** Why do you think 'full of' is repeated in line 4?
    b What effect does it have?
4 'Stand and deliver' and 'your money or your life' are both phrases associated with highway robbers. How does this fit with the ideas in the first stanza?
5 The weather is 'ugly'.
  a What exactly is the weather like, and how do you know?
  b How does the weather seem to change in the poem?
6   **a** What is 'a bandolier of light', do you think?
    b Why do you think McCaig chooses this as the last phrase of the poem?

GradeStudio

Sample answer ⓑ

To achieve a B on this AO2 descriptor, you need to show **thoughtful consideration of ideas/themes**. The following extract from a sample answer would hit the grade B requirement.

> Nature in the poem is dangerous, full of 'threats' and 'dark light', but it also gladdens the heart and is a source of 'enrichment'. The mountains are 'marvellous', in the end.

Words/phrases to explore (AO1 and AO2)

Activity 2

1 'My life was enriched/with an infusion of theirs'. Now you have looked at the whole poem, how do you think the poet's life has been 'enriched' by the experience?
2 Why do you think the first five words are on a line of their own? These two lines could have been at the end of the poem. Why do you think McCaig places them here?

Comparing with other poems

Activity 3

1 **Comparing ideas and themes**
Compare the threats presented by the places in 'Below the Green Corrie' and 'Wind'.
2 **Comparing writers' devices**
Compare the ways in which the writers of 'Below the Green Corrie' and 'The Prelude' present mountains.

▶ Poem Glossary

subjugated subdued

Storm in the Black Forest

by D.H. Lawrence

Read the poem in your AQA Anthology, then complete the
activities below.

Initial responses

Activity 1

1 'Jugfull after jugfull' begins the **imagery** of liquid in the poem. Read
   carefully through the rest of the poem, jotting down all the other
   examples of liquid imagery you can find.
2 Look at the nine words beginning 'white liquid'.
   a Which vowel sound is repeated again and again here? (This is
      called **assonance**.)
   b Why do you think the writer does this?
   c Now look at the whole two lines beginning 'jugfull'. What other
      repetitions are there?
3 a After the short line 'and is gone', what has disappeared from the
      poem, apart from the lightning itself? Think about the work you
      did in answering the last question.
   b What is the effect of the short line?
4 The comparison of the lightning to a 'white snake' appears in line 7.
   a How is the idea of the snake continued?
   b Which assonance appears here?
5 What other suggestion of something inhuman appears in this **stanza**?
6 Why do you think the line beginning 'And the rain' is a single line?
7 There are three exclamation marks in the last four lines. Why do
   you think the writer does this?

Words/phrases to explore (AO1 and AO2)

Activity 2

In what ways is it suggested in the poem that this electricity, which is a
force of nature, cannot be easily 'subjugated'? Think about the imagery
in the poem.

Comparing with other poems

Activity 3

1 **Comparing ideas and themes**
   Compare the violent weather in 'Storm in the Black Forest'
   and 'Wind'.
2 **Comparing writers' devices**
   Compare the ways in which violent weather is presented in 'Storm
   in the Black Forest' and 'Wind'.

GradeStudio

Sample answer Ⓐ*

To achieve an A* on this AO2
descriptor, you need to show
**evaluation of writers' uses of
language and/or structure and/
or form and their effects on
readers**. The following extract
from a sample answer would hit
the grade A* requirement.

Activity I, question 2
The assonance of 'i'
sounds in lines 2 and
3 switches from long to
short sounds and back
again, in a dizzying
pattern, the high vowel
sounds being perfect for
the flashing lightning
high in the air. With
the added repetition
of 'jugfull' and the
reappearance of the
assonance in the second
stanza, it might seem
as though Lawrence
is overdoing it; but
perhaps that's the point.
It is overpowering.

Wind

by Ted Hughes

Read the poem in your AQA Anthology, then complete the activities below.

GradeStudio

Sample answer Ⓐ

To achieve an A* on this AO2 descriptor, you need to show **convincing/imaginative interpretation of ideas/themes**. To do this, you need to work hard on your view of the ideas in the poem. The following extract from a sample answer would hit the grade A* requirement.

Activity 1, question 4

The wind seems not just powerful, but malevolent, and almost supernatural. It is no wonder that the people in the house seem transfixed with fear. Outside 'the lens of a mad eye' seems to have fallen on them. This is a power from which nature itself seems to 'stampede', and which deals acts of wanton destruction and torture, as a gull is tortured in mid-air, it would seem. Now inanimate stones shriek in horror, and the thing is about to break through the terrified window.

Initial responses | Activity 1

1 **a** What is the house being compared to in the first line?
   b What other two things is it compared to in the last two **stanzas**?
2 Jot down all the action words in the first stanza. What things here are made to seem alive, which aren't usually?
3 How does the writer use light in the second stanza? Look for what the light does, as well as the colours.
4 How does the writer suggest the strength of the wind in the third stanza? Look for at least three things.
5 Why do you think the fields seem to be 'quivering'?
6 Look carefully at the **enjambment** in the fourth stanza – the way 'black-/Back' is split over two lines. What effect does this create here?
7 In the last stanza, inanimate things are **personified** again – given living qualities, as in the first stanza. How many can you find? Jot them down.

Words/phrases to explore (AO1 and AO2) | Activity 2

Look again at the line beginning 'The tent of the hills'. Analyse this **metaphor** carefully – why the hills are being compared to a tent and a guyrope, how sight and sound are being used.

Comparing with other poems | Activity 3

1 **Comparing ideas and themes**
   Compare the threats presented by nature in 'Wind' and 'The Prelude'.
2 **Comparing writers' devices**
   Compare the ways in which place is presented in 'Wind' and 'Price We Pay for the Sun'.

Looking at the poems individually: what have you learned?

My learning ▶

In this section you will:
● think about which poems interested you most and why.

Complete Activities 1 and 2 below. As you do, think about which poems and which features of poems were most interesting to you. If you're working with someone else, you could learn from each other, or consider what differences in choices might reveal about you as readers.

Note that the words in bold in the tasks below refer to the key words in the Assessment Objectives.

Assessment Objective 1 (AO1)

Activity 1

1   Which of these poems did you **respond** to most strongly? You may have liked it, or disliked it, or found it the most interesting, or horrible. You may have a number of things to say about it.
    Working with a partner, or by yourself, display your responses as a spider diagram, and then compare it with someone else's, to see if you have responded to the poems in similar ways.

2   Which poems did you find it easiest to offer an **interpretation** about? In other words, you had a view about a poem's meaning that you could argue from the text and **select detail** to support your view. For instance, you might have found it easy to argue and support the view that the speaker in 'Spellbound' is suffering a breakdown.
    Suggesting more than one interpretation of a poem, or parts of a poem, gives you opportunities to score more marks. For instance, there are several ways in which you could interpret the nature of the mountains in the excerpt from 'The Prelude'.

Assessment Objective 2 (AO2)

Activity 2

1   Which features of **language**, **structure** or **form** did you understand best? The most promising ones to write about in the exam will be the ones where you have most to say. For instance, you might have found several things to say about:
    ● the effect of personification in 'Below the Green Corrie' (language)
    ● the way 'The Blackbird of Glanmore' leads to the final isolated line (structure)
    ● the effects of the change to full rhyme at the end of 'Cold Knap Lake' (form).
    When answering this question, it would be best if you chose your own examples rather than using the ones above!

2   What **ideas** did you identify in the poems? Again, the best answers will probably identify several ideas in a poem, or several aspects of one idea. For instance, you might have identified or explored more than one idea about society in 'London'.

In this section you will learn how to:
● compare poems and address the Assessment Objectives
● develop writing skills and practise exam-style questions.

Assessment Objective:

The Assessment Objective you will be focusing on in this part of the chapter is:

AO3 make comparisons and explain links between texts, evaluating writers' different ways of expressing meaning and achieving effects.

Comparing the 'Place' poems

Assessment Objective 3 is broken into two parts:

▶ comparing ideas and themes in the poems, with detail

▶ comparing the ways writers use language or structure or form, with detail.

In responding to the exam question, you will need to address both these parts.

Comparing ideas and themes

Read the poems 'Cold Knap Lake' and 'The Wild Swans at Coole', then complete the activities below.

Activity 1

Thinking about ideas and themes in the two poems, list as many similarities and differences as you can. For example: both poems are about memories of earlier events and suggest that the **speakers** are aware that they are getting older.

Activity 2

Using your lists of similarities and differences from Activity 1, decide how different the poems are for each point you made. For example, 'The Wild Swans at Coole' seems full of sadness for lost times. What things does the speaker seem to have lost? Has the speaker in 'Cold Knap Lake' lost anything? What?

Use quotations or refer to specific parts of the poem to support what you think.

Activity 3

Find a detail from each poem that you could compare directly. For example:

> scatter wheeling in great broken rings
> Upon their clamorous wings

(The Wild Swans at Coole)

> the treading, heavy webs of swans
> as their wings beat and whistle on the air

(Cold Knap Lake)

Write two or three paragraphs exploring all the similarities and differences you can find, asking yourself:
● Which statement seems more active? Why?
● What sense is used in the second detail that isn't in the first? Why?
● How does each detail fit into the poem as a whole?

Sample answer B

To achieve a B on this AO3 descriptor, you need to make a **developed comparison of ideas and/or meanings and/or techniques.** The following extract from a sample answer to the task in Activity 3 would hit the grade B requirement.

Both poems describe swans in similar ways, but with very different purposes. Both describe the sight and sound of the swans in flight, though the description in 'The Wild Swans at Coole' is more visual and complete: it is easy to picture the swans as they 'scatter' in 'rings', 'wheeling' – Clarke only gives the sound of the wings, so we have to imagine them 'on the air'. 'The heavy webs of swans' is more exact than anything in the other poem, though, because Clarke wants to show the effect the swans have on the water as they fly up. 'All suddenly mount' in 'Wild Swans' is much more general.

Comparing writers' methods

Now you need to think about the similarities and differences in terms of the methods the writers use, and why they use them. For these two poems, you could say:

▶ both use swans to describe memory

▶ both switch between the past and the present

▶ 'The Wild Swans at Coole' uses regular **stanzas** and a regular rhyme scheme whereas 'Cold Knap Lake' uses irregular stanzas and some half-rhymes, and then a full rhyme at the end.

These are fairly simple links, though, rather than comparisons which explore or analyse.

Better marks can usually be achieved by taking two details or quotations which have some similarity and exploring them.

Activity 4

Look at:
* the last four lines of 'The Wild Swans at Coole'
* the last two lines of 'Cold Knap Lake'.

Explore the similarities and differences between these details:

1 The last two lines of 'Cold Knap Lake' are separated from the rest of the poem. Why do you think Clarke does this?

2 One of these is a statement, but the other is a question. What difference does it make? Why do the poets choose to end like this?

3 The last two lines of every **stanza** of 'Wild Swans' **rhyme**, including this one, but the rhyme at the end of 'Cold Knap Lake' is the only one in the poem. Why? What things is each of the poets connecting together with rhyme?

You should have found a lot of things to say, to form the basis of a detailed comparison. Choosing details about which you have plenty to say is a key skill for the exam.

GradeStudio

Sample answer A*

To achieve an A* on this AO3 descriptor, you need to make an **evaluative comparison of writers' uses of language and/or structure and/or form and their effects on readers, with detail.** The following extract from a sample answer to the task in Activity 4 would hit the grade A* requirement.

Both poems end with a rhyming couplet, but the effects are quite different. 'Wild Swans' ends with a question, and one which flows quite naturally from the rest of the thoughts in the poem: having watched the swans in the past and now, the speaker thinks about the future. Given the world-weary feel of his present, death could be in his mind. The rhythm of the poem is not broken, though: each stanza has had the same lines and ended in the same way. 'Cold Knap Lake' is quite different, because the two lines are separated from the rest of the poem, and the rhyme is a new, almost jarring feature.

It reads almost like a nursery rhyme, accentuated by nursery-rhyme figures such as the 'poor man's daughter' and the mysterious swans, unlike the matter-of-fact quality of the ending of 'Wild Swans'. The sounds repeated by the final rhymes have quite different effects, too. The 'a' sounds in 'away' and 'day' seem high and uplifting like the swans, despite the undercurrent of death, but the feminine endings and lower sound of 'water' and 'daughter' seem to drag this final statement down. These lines act as a conclusion to an argument, in a way: all memories are dragged down into the lake of forgetfulness.

Putting it all together

To practise the skills you have been working on in these comparison activities, here are two more activities on a different pair of poems: 'Below the Green Corrie' and the extract from 'The Prelude'.

Activity 5

1   What ideas and themes can you find in the poems which are similar?

   a   Both the poems are about people alone in a natural surrounding. What attitudes to nature can you find in the poems?

   b   What similarities and differences are there in the type of threat that nature seems to make?

   c   What are the effects on the **speakers** of their experiences? List as many similarities and differences as you can.

2   Now you have a list of similarities and differences between the two poems, you can consider how similar they are, or how different. For instance, the mountains seem to threaten both speakers, but how different are the threats? Do the threats stay or not? For how long? Include some detail or evidence to support each point.

3 Find a detail from each poem that you could compare directly, for example:

> Their leader
> swaggered up close in the dark light
> full of threats, full of thunders.

(Below the Green Corrie)

> with purpose of its own
> And measured motion like a living thing
> Strode after me.

(The Prelude)

The simple link between the two details above is that they both describe the mountains apparently moving towards the **speakers**. However, to reach the grades you are aiming for, you need to explore all the similarities and differences you can find between the details. So here you would need to consider:

- Which seems more threatening, and why?
- What type of movement does each seem to make?
- How do the speakers in each poem seem to react to the movement?
- How does each detail fit into the poems as a whole?

Once you have chosen your two details, write two paragraphs comparing them.

GradeStudio

Sample answer Ⓐ

To achieve an A on this AO3 descriptor, you need to make an **analytical comparison of ideas and/or meanings and/or techniques**. The following extract from a sample answer to the task in Activity 5 would hit the grade A requirement.

Both speakers appear to be threatened directly by the mountains around them. In 'Below the Green Corrie' the mountain is surrounded with darkness ('dark light', 'thunders') like a pantomime villain, whereas Wordsworth is not as specific as this. The mountain in 'Green Corrie' 'swaggered', which suggests the mountain is aware of its own power, but in Wordsworth it 'strode', suggesting a faster and more threatening power. The power of nature appears to swagger up 'close' to the speaker in 'Green Corrie', but in Wordsworth 'after me' suggests that the speaker is actually retreating in terror – which indeed he is.

Comparing writers' methods and purposes

Compare the ways in which the two writers personify the mountains. Discuss or make notes on:

- what each **personification** suggests about the nature of the mountains
- what different sorts of threat are suggested, and how
- how the personifications create different **tones** in the poems.

GradeStudio

Sample answer B

To achieve a B on this AO3 descriptor, you need to make a **developed comparison of ideas and/or meanings and/or techniques**. The following extract from a sample answer to the task in Activity 6 would hit the grade B requirement.

The personifications in both poems suggest that the mountains are powerful and aggressive, as they are 'like bandits' that 'swaggered', and they 'gathered round me' ('Below the Green Corrie') and in 'The Prelude' they have 'voluntary power' and 'towered up between me and the stars'. These are different types of personification, though. In 'Below the Green Corrie' the comparison is very specific. The mountains are described as 'bandits' throughout: they were 'prowlers' who 'swaggered' wearing a 'bandolier' and 'swashbuckling'. Wordsworth is not as specific as this, and the mountains seem more threatening for being unknown: they are 'like a living thing' and 'unknown modes of being', 'mighty forms'.

Writing in the exam

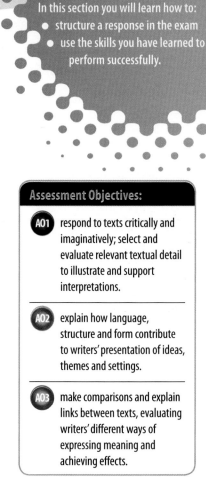

In this section you will learn how to:
- structure a response in the exam
- use the skills you have learned to perform successfully.

Planning and writing your response

When faced with any exam question your approach should be: Read, Think, Write, Edit.

Read

Read the questions and choose quickly which one to answer based on the poem that is named, or on what each question is asking you to do.

Think

This is the planning stage so don't start writing straight away. Think about the question carefully first! The first word of the exam task is likely to be 'compare' so you should build your response around a comparison of the two poems. You should establish a comparative framework such as the one on page 58 before you write. Within it, jot down ideas from the poems, and one or two details that you're planning to use. Choose things that you can write quite a lot about.

This whole process should take no more than 5 minutes (and not less than 2) as you only have 45 minutes for the whole task.

Write

When you write, you must show: what you think about the poems; why they are written in the ways they are; and what happens when you compare the poems, or parts of them (i.e. the things the Assessment Objectives focus on). The phrase 'or parts of them' is important. Don't write everything you know about the poems. Instead, select from what you know to write about the poems in a way that answers the question.

Edit

If you have any time left, you should look for ways to improve your answer. Could you add another meaning of a word or phrase? Is there another effect of a writer's choice of language? Additions of this kind might gain an extra mark.

Assessment Objectives:

AO1 respond to texts critically and imaginatively; select and evaluate relevant textual detail to illustrate and support interpretations.

AO2 explain how language, structure and form contribute to writers' presentation of ideas, themes and settings.

AO3 make comparisons and explain links between texts, evaluating writers' different ways of expressing meaning and achieving effects.

Putting it into practice

Let's take a typical exam question:

Compare (AO3) the ways in which weather (AO1) is presented (AO2) in 'Storm in the Black Forest' and one other poem from 'Place'.

Let's suppose that you chose 'Wind' as a good poem to compare with 'Storm in the Black Forest' – both are about storms, use a range of devices, and deal with a relationship between humans and nature, though they are very different.

First, you need to jot down a few ideas from the poems that you're going to use when you write. For example:

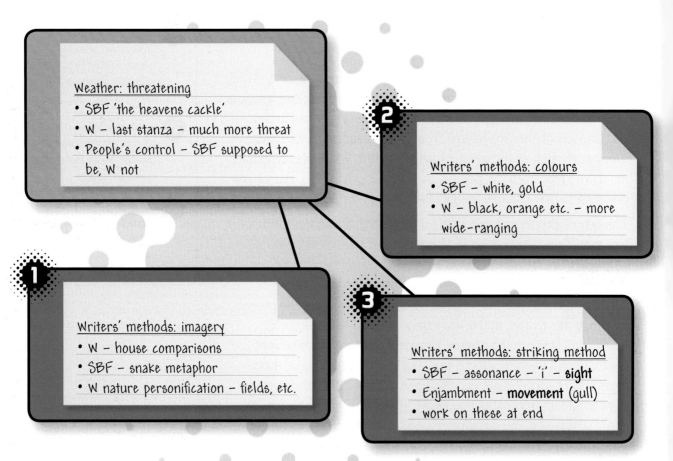

Weather: threatening
- SBF 'the heavens cackle'
- W – last stanza – much more threat
- People's control – SBF supposed to be, W not

2 **Writers' methods: colours**
- SBF – white, gold
- W – black, orange etc. – more wide-ranging

1 **Writers' methods: imagery**
- W – house comparisons
- SBF – snake metaphor
- W nature personification – fields, etc.

3 **Writers' methods: striking method**
- SBF – assonance – 'i' – **sight**
- Enjambment – **movement** (gull)
- work on these at end

In the notes above, the student decided that the weather in each poem was very threatening, so that might be a good place to start, but the poems were very different in method, so the rest of the response could be structured around different methods. Three ideas about method is plenty: the task is not to try to offer an exhaustive account – you are just showing off your thinking and writing skills.

After thinking of the three methods, the student decided which order to write about the methods in (indicated by the numbers). Having decided on this structure, the student decided that an opening paragraph showing what she was going to say would help the reader. Often this is unnecessary, but here she could start work on all three Assessment Objectives quickly.

GradeStudio

Read the extracts from these sample student answers, together with the question below and the examiner comments. You could then try the sample exam question at the end.

Compare the ways in which weather is presented in 'Storm in the Black Forest' and one other poem from 'Place'.

Openings

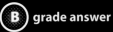

B grade answer

Student A

The weather presented in these poems seems very similar, in some ways. It is extreme, with huge amounts of lightning in 'Storm in the Black Forest' and a wind that seems like a hurricane in 'Wind'. Both situations seem very threatening, but much more so in 'Wind', where the human beings are terrified. The methods used by the poets are similar in some ways, with extensive use of imagery, but the most striking use of technique is different in each poem.

Examiner comment

Student A is already showing that there is going to be a **developed comparison** of both ideas and methods (18–24, grade B).

A* grade answer

Student B

These are poems with very different intentions. 'Storm in the Black Forest', through its presentation of the power of lightning, is set on questioning the limits of people's power, and their arrogance. 'Wind', on the other hand, seems to have no such defining idea; rather, it simply focuses on the terrifying natural strength of the wind and its multiple effects. The methods the poets choose follow the same pattern, in a way: Lawrence single-mindedly uses one central technique in describing the lightning, whereas Hughes employs a much wider armoury.

Examiner comment

Student B gets on with scoring even more quickly, showing an **exploratory response** (25–30, grade A) to the ideas in the poems, and some sense of **evaluative comparison** (31–36, grade A*).

Examiner comment

Both these openings start to achieve in all three Assessment Objectives by getting straight on with the task. They avoid using 'In this essay I am going to write about... ' which is a waste of time. It is worth noting that they could not have written their subsequent paragraphs without doing the thinking shown in these openings first.

GradeStudio

A paragraph on an idea

B grade answer

Student A

In the last stanza of 'Wind' the people in the house being battered by the wind are 'gripped' by fear, and cannot move or think. They are shaken by the house, which seems to have taken on a life of its own, and by the windows which 'tremble to come in', suggesting not only the physical shaking caused by the wind but the idea of a malevolent presence about to enter. If there is a threat in 'Storm in the Black Forest', it is unspoken, apart from the unearthly idea that 'the heavens cackle'. At the same time, Lawrence makes it clear that humans, who are supposed to have 'subjugated' the elements, clearly have not, so in that sense it is like 'Wind', where people have no control at all over the wind.

Examiner comment

In Student A's response, the two ideas offered about the windows hit **thoughtful consideration** and the two comparisons developed around threat hit **developed comparison in terms of ideas/themes**, so two descriptors in the 18–24 mark band have been hit.

A* grade answer

Student B

Lawrence's poem seems to admire and even celebrate the strength of the lightning, and its strange, crackling light, which has nothing to do with people: it is compared to a 'snake' and the heavens 'cackle with uncouth sounds'. These establish the lightning as beyond people's power, even though they think they have 'chained' electricity. The repeated 'supposed to!' shows people's arrogance in thinking this. This is a conceptual idea about weather which 'Wind' does not try to encompass. Humans are simply victims in 'Wind', at the mercy of the elements, unable to function in the face of its power. They are not alone in this: even the fields, the trees and the hills are battered by it.

Examiner comment

Student B hits descriptors in higher bands. There is an **exploration of ideas** (25–30) here, and some **evaluative comparison** (31–36).

A paragraph comparing two details

B grade answer

Student A

Lawrence uses a lot of assonance in lines 2 and 3. Both long and short 'i' sounds are repeated, so it's like the light flickering, or going on and off. 'Jugfull after jugfull' comes before this, so the effect of both together is quite relentless. In 'Wind' Hughes doesn't use this device, but uses a lot of others, such as enjambment in 'a black-/Back gull bent slowly'.

Examiner comment

Student A makes two connected points about the use of assonance, so hits **appreciation of writers' uses of language** (18–24). The comparison is really only a simple link, and the language comment on 'Wind' is also at a much lower level.

A* grade answer

Student B

The assonance of 'i' sounds in lines 2 and 3 switches from long to short sounds and back again, in a dizzying pattern, the high vowel sounds being perfect for the flashing lightning high in the air. With the added repetition of 'jugfull' and the reappearance of the assonance in the second stanza, it might seem as though Lawrence is overdoing it; but perhaps that's the point. It is overpowering. Hughes, on the other hand, uses a whole range of techniques rather than this hammering of assonance, but is equally clever in capturing sight for the reader, as the break of 'black-/Back' seems to capture the excruciating slow bending of the gull in the power of the wind, as though it was being slowly broken in two. The Lawrence device is clever: so is this, but it's horrifying too. 'Wind' is a poem of feelings, not ideas.

Examiner comment

Student B achieves a lot more, by being willing to spend a lot more time analysing the details chosen. Their comments on 'Storm in the Black Forest' move from **analytical** to **evaluative** (31–36), and they then not only repeat this skill with the comments on the line break, but produce **evaluative selection of a range of detail integrated into comparison**. Two 31–36 descriptors have been met.

You are now ready to tackle an exam question. Here's one to try:

Compare the unpleasant effects of nature shown in 'Neighbours' and one other poem from 'Place'.

When you've written your answer, you could mark it, or get a partner to mark it, using the mark scheme on page 134.

My learning ▶

In this section you will learn how to:
● become familiar with the poems as a whole
● start to make links between the poems.

Getting to know the poems

The poems

Flag	**At the Border**	**Bayonet Charge**
John Agard	*Choman Hardi*	*Ted Hughes*
Out of the Blue (extract)	**Belfast Confetti**	**The Falling Leaves**
Simon Armitage	*Ciaran Carson*	*Margaret Postgate Cole*
Mametz Wood	**Poppies**	**Come On, Come Back**
Owen Sheers	*Jane Weir*	*Stevie Smith*
The Yellow Palm	**Futility**	**next to of course god america**
Robert Minhinnick	*Wilfred Owen*	*e.e. cummings*
The Right Word	**The Charge of the Light Brigade**	**Hawk Roosting**
Imtiaz Dharker	*Alfred, Lord Tennyson*	*Ted Hughes*

Assessment Objectives:

 AO1 respond to texts critically and imaginatively; select and evaluate relevant textual detail to illustrate and support interpretations.

AO2 explain how language, structure and form contribute to writers' presentation of ideas, themes and settings.

AO3 make comparisons and explain links between texts, evaluating writers' different ways of expressing meaning and achieving effects.

The poems in this chapter are centred around conflict between countries and people, which produces violence and death. All the poems are in your AQA Anthology.

In this chapter you will be:

▶ looking at the individual poems

▶ comparing the poems

▶ learning how to approach exam questions.

As a result of this preparation you will be developing your writing skills in order to hit the Assessment Objectives. See page v for more information about what the Assessment Objectives mean. In the exam you will have to compare two poems from this chapter.

Getting started

The first thing to do is to start to familiarise yourself with the 'Conflict' poems. You can do the following activities by yourself, or in a group.

Activity 1

Read all the 'Conflict' poems in your AQA Anthology, quickly. Just notice what they seem to be about – don't worry about trying to make sense of every line.

Activity 2

Now find as many links as you can between some of the poems. You will need a large piece of paper with some headings on. Below is a list of ways you could look at the poems. You could use some of these to form your headings, though you could think of some of your own as well.

Ways to look at the poems	Tips on what to watch out for
What the poems are about	All the poems are about conflict – but what sort? If they belong to a particular war or time, which one? Does the attitude to conflict seem to be angry/regretful/accepting? Which poems seem to have similar attitudes?
Beginnings/endings	Any similarities? How about lines that look a bit similar, but where there's a difference too? For example, both 'Come On, Come Back' and 'The Charge of the Light Brigade' use repeated phrases at the end. How are they similar or different in effect?
Length	You might notice some distinct similarities or differences. Include the number and length of **stanzas**, if there are any.
Rhyme	You need to look a little more carefully now. Is there a regular **rhyme scheme**? Does it change? Be careful – some poems that don't seem to **rhyme** often use a lot of **half-rhyme** or **echoes**, like 'Futility', or might suddenly rhyme. Look at 'Mametz Wood', for example; there's a strong rhyme in the last three lines, but not before. If you were working on this poem, you'd need to think about why the writer does this.
Rhythm	Are there any poems with a strong **rhythm**, such as 'The Charge of the Light Brigade'? Are any of the others similar to this?
Language	Some of these poems make considerable use of repetition of words and phrases, but others hardly use repetition at all. Look for repetition in each poem. What effect does it have? If there is no repetition, why do you think the writer made that choice?
Imagery	Some poems are rich in **imagery**, such as **metaphors** and **similes**, while others might seem quite plain. Make a note of some obvious similarities and differences.

Now that you have found a lot of links, try displaying your findings in a different way, on a sheet of A3. Working on your own, in a pair or in a group, you could try any of the following ways.

1 Spread the titles out on the sheet and draw links between them, labelling each one.

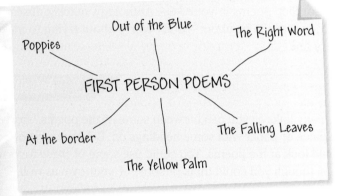

2 Draw a picture or symbol for each idea (such as death or nature) that appears in more than one poem, and group the poems around each – a poem can appear in more than one group.

3 Draw a picture, or pictures, for each poem on the sheet, and link similar ones with arrows.

In these activities you have started to tackle all three Assessment Objectives. Now you will be focusing on AO1 and AO2 as you look at the poems individually (pages 65–81). You will return to AO3 when you compare the poems (pages 82–85). Finally, you will look at how to turn your knowledge and skills into successful exam answers, before you attempt one yourself (pages 86–91).

Looking at the poems individually

Looking at the poems individually

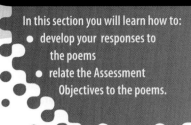

My learning ▶

In this section you will learn how to:
- develop your responses to the poems
- relate the Assessment Objectives to the poems.

This section of the chapter, pages 65–81, is designed to lead you through an exploration of each individual poem. Throughout, you will find examples of student responses at different levels.

In the exam, you will have to write about the poems individually as well as comparing them.

In the exam you have to compare two poems; one named poem and one unnamed poem, which means you can choose the second one. On the Higher Tier paper the following will not be named poems: 'Flag', 'The Right Word', 'The Falling Leaves'. Of course, you could choose any of these poems to compare with the named one.

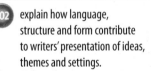

Assessment Objectives:

The Assessment Objectives you will be focusing on in this part of the chapter are:

AO1 respond to texts critically and imaginatively; select and evaluate relevant textual detail to illustrate and support interpretations.

AO2 explain how language, structure and form contribute to writers' presentation of ideas, themes and settings.

Flag

by John Agard

Read the poem in your AQA Anthology, then complete the activities below.

Examiner tip

Poetic devices
In the exam, you should refer to poetic devices, such as **metaphor** or **simile**, and other terms carefully and correctly. Terms in **bold** are explained in the Glossary of Poetic Devices (page 137).

Sample answer **B**

To achieve a B on this AO1 descriptor, you need to make a **considered response**. To do this, you need to think about more than one thing. The following extract from a sample answer would hit the grade B requirement.

> Activity 2
>
> The message of the poem is a simple one, that fighting for a flag means having to 'blind your conscience', but it is also shown as very tempting, as it's very powerful – it can give you power, courage and fame.

Initial responses
Activity 1

1 Look at the first four **stanzas**. Identify the active words in the opening lines in each of the stanzas. Why do you think Agard has chosen to make the flag seem active?
2 'Just a piece of cloth' is a small thing that actually has great power. How is the power reflected in each of the last lines of the stanzas?
3 What are the various realities about war that are suggested in some of the last lines of the stanzas?
4 Why would the **speaker's** 'friend' want 'such a cloth'?
5 Why do you think 'Just' has been placed at the beginning of the line in the last stanza, when it isn't in the other stanzas?

Words/phrases to explore (AO1)
Activity 2

Why exactly do you have to 'blind your conscience to the end' if you possess the power that the flag can give? Look at all the things the flag is said to give in the poem.

Comparing with other poems
Activity 3

1 **Comparing ideas and themes**
   Compare the attitudes of the voices to conflict in 'Flag' and 'next to of course god america'.
2 **Comparing writers' devices**
   Compare the use of repeated words and phrases in 'Flag' and 'The Charge of the Light Brigade'.

Out of the Blue (extract)

by Simon Armitage

Read the poem in your AQA Anthology, then complete the activities below.

Initial responses

Activity 1

1 The man in the building is waving a white shirt. What different things does he imagine the onlooker might see this as?
2 There are lots of repetitions in this poem: of words, sentence forms and letters at the beginning of words (**alliteration**). Go through and pick them all out. This will help you to notice where the patterns vary.
3 The man on the ledge is clearly desperate. Find places in the poem where you can see or hear this – think about the sounds and patterns of the words as well as what they mean.
4 In the fourth **stanza** there is a **personification**.
   a What is personified, and why?
   b How does it make the reader feel the effect on the man on the ledge?
5 In the fifth stanza there is a change in the pattern of punctuation, when there is a full stop before the end of the second line. What is the effect of this, do you think?
6 In the sixth stanza, there is another change in pattern. You expect the repetition of 'believing' to be on the same line, but it is put on the next line by itself – the only one-word line. Why do you think Armitage has done this?
7 The last two lines form the only **rhyming couplet** in the poem.
   a Why does Armitage do this at the end?
   b What are the two meanings of the last word?

Words/phrases to explore (AO1 and AO2)

Activity 2

'My love' in the last line identifies the onlooker for the first time.
1 Why does Armitage wait until this moment to mention this?
2 What effect does it have on the feeling of the poem as a whole?
   Try to suggest more than one point.

Comparing poems

Activity 3

1 **Comparing ideas and themes**
   Compare the ways in which the feelings of an individual in danger are shown in 'Out of the Blue' and 'The Right Word'.
2 **Comparing writers' devices**
   Compare the ways in which desperation is conveyed in 'Out of the Blue' and 'Belfast Confetti'.

GradeStudio

Context

The poem refers to the people who were trapped in the burning twin towers in New York in the 9/11 attack, and who jumped to their death from the buildings.

GradeStudio

Sample answer B

To achieve a B on this AO2 descriptor, you need to show **appreciation/consideration of the writers' uses of language and/or form and/or structure**. To do this, you need to do more than just explain an effect, which is Band 4. The following extract from a sample answer would hit the grade B requirement.

> In the last stanza, the pattern returns again with the repetition of 'tiring', which makes the reader feel that the man is running out of energy to protest, but also that the poem itself is running out of space and time – you can see the end.

Context

Mametz Wood In the First World War Battle of the Somme in July 1916, the 38th Welsh Division attacked the German positions in Mametz Wood. The wood was taken, but 4,000 Welsh troops perished.

▶ Poem Glossary

dance-macabre a medieval idea of a dance of death, in which Death leads a row of dancing figures to the grave

stands sentinel stands guard, like a sentry

Sample answer Ⓐ

To achieve an A* on this AO1 descriptor, you need to show an **insightful exploratory response**. To do this, you need to explore effectively ideas in the text. The following extract from a sample answer would hit the grade A* requirement.

> **Activity 1, question 7**
> In the last stanza, the voices of the dead soldiers seem to rise from the opened grave as the earth is pushed away. But the restoration hinted at earlier in the poem is a false perspective: the notes 'slip away' from the shattered faces, as though the corpses are dribbling the notes of a dirge.

Mametz Wood

by Owen Sheers

Read the poem in your AQA Anthology, then complete the activities below.

Initial responses

Activity 1

1. What different times are mentioned in the poem?
2. How does Sheers emphasise the fragility of life in the second **stanza**? Why does he compare the skull to 'a blown/and broken bird's egg'?
3. Why do you think Sheers describes the earth as 'standing sentinel'?
4. Work out the idea that Sheers has about the earth in the fourth stanza.
5. Where in the poem can you find ideas about restoration of what has been damaged?
6. Work out exactly the appearance of the twenty bodies.
7. What seems to be happening in the last stanza? What effect does this have on the reader?
8. Find the **rhyme** in the last stanza. Why do you think Sheers uses rhyme here?

Words/phrases to explore (AO1 and AO2)

Activity 2

Bearing in mind what you've found in answering the questions in Activity 1, answer the following questions.

1. What can you say about the phrase 'the wasted young' in the second line?
2. How does the idea of 'wasted' appear in the poem as a whole? Try to suggest more than one point.

Comparing poems

Activity 3

1. **Comparing ideas and themes**
   Compare the attitudes of the **speakers** to dead soldiers in 'Mametz Wood' and 'Futility'.
2. **Comparing writers' devices**
   Compare the ways in which death is presented in 'The Falling Leaves' and 'Mametz Wood'.

The Yellow Palm

by Robert Minhinnick

Read the poem in your AQA Anthology, then complete the activities below.

▶ **Poem Glossary**

Palestine Street a street in Baghdad

muezzin the muezzin in a mosque calls the faithful to prayer

The Mother of all Wars Saddam Hussein referred to the first Gulf War against the Allied forces as 'The Mother of all Wars'

salaam a respectful greeting

Initial responses

Activity 1

1 Each of the first five **stanzas** contains a contrast of some sort. Read through each stanza quickly, looking for the contrasts.

2 In the first stanza, how does the writer stress the fragility of life?

3 In the second stanza, you could find more than one contrast. Think about:
   • colours
   • what the muezzin should be feeling, and what he is feeling
   • how the **rhyme** stresses the second contrast.

4 In the third stanza, how does Minhinnick show the difference between what the men he meets are, and what they were? Look for more than one example.

5 In the fourth stanza, even nature seems to be part of the war. How does Minhinnick suggest this? Look for the words he uses as well as ideas.

6 In the fifth stanza, how is something dangerous made to seem not dangerous? What is the irony about the word 'blessed'?

7 The last stanza does not seem to have a contrast, but there are several ways to interpret it.
   a Is this a good thing that happens, or not?
   b The beggar child is given something he hasn't asked for. What is it, and how does he get it? Think about what is happening in the previous stanza.

Words/phrases to explore (AO1 and AO2)

Activity 2

1 What effect does the last line have on the reader?

2 Depending on how you interpret the last line, what effect does it have on how the reader sees the 'message' of the whole poem?

Comparing poems

Activity 3

1 **Comparing ideas and themes**
   Compare the effects of war in a city in 'The Yellow Palm' and 'Belfast Confetti'.

2 **Comparing writers' devices**
   Compare the effects of repeated lines and stanza forms in 'The Yellow Palm' and 'The Charge of the Light Brigade'.

GradeStudio

Sample answer **B**

To achieve a B on this AO2 descriptor, you need to show **thoughtful consideration of ideas/themes**. To do this, you need to think of more than one idea about the poem. The following extract from a sample answer would hit the grade B requirement.

> The war has destroyed the soldiers' lives, making them into beggars; but this is made to seem sharper by the soldiers, who were not just guards but 'Imperial' Guards, being now blind, and ironically giving their soldiers' salutes in return for alms.

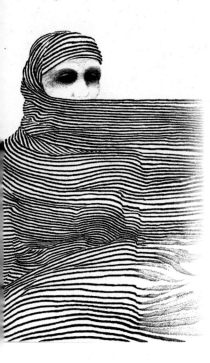

The Right Word

by Imtiaz Dharker

Read the poem in your AQA Anthology, then complete the activities below.

Initial responses

Activity 1

1. **a** Identify the different words used to describe the figure in the shadows, starting with 'terrorist'.
   b The word 'shadow' is repeated several times. Why do you think the writer does this?
2. Identify the different things the figure is doing in the shadows, beginning with 'lurking'.
3. 'Words' are mentioned three times in the poem. Find these, and notice how they form a progression in the poem.
4. The poem changes in the fifth **stanza**.
   a How does the first line connect with the description of the figure here?
   b How does the figure become clearer here, and more dangerous?
5. How does the first line of the sixth stanza show the state of mind of the **speaker**?
6. Why do you think the speaker uses the word 'lost' in the sixth stanza?
7. Who do you think the 'you' might be at the beginning of the seventh stanza?
8. **a** How is the last stanza a surprise, after the rest of the poem? Think about the changes in **form** as well as the change of feeling.
   b What is the effect of the last line? Think about what has been restored.

GradeStudio

Sample answer **B**

To achieve a B on this AO1 descriptor, you need to show **details linked to interpretation**. To do this, you need to link details to your view of what the poem is about. The following extract from a sample answer would hit the grade B requirement.

> The feeling of the poem changes in the last stanza to one of respect and civilised, peaceful behaviour. The invitation 'Come in' is repeated and the frightening figure actually 'steps in' and 'carefully' removes shoes, suggesting respect and regard for the people in the house.

Words/phrases to explore (AO1)

Activity 2

Having worked through the questions above, think about the sentence 'Are words no more/than waving, wavering flags?' How are the ideas here found in the poem as a whole? Think about the meaning of each of the last three words of the sentence.

Comparing poems

Activity 3

1. **Comparing ideas and themes**
   Compare how the two sides of conflict are shown in 'The Right Word' and 'At the Border'.
2. **Comparing writers' devices**
   Compare the effects of repeated form in 'The Right Word' and 'Flag'.

At the Border

by Choman Hardi

Read the poem in your AQA Anthology, then complete the activities below.

Initial responses

Activity 1

1 'It is your last check-in point in this country!' What do the words and punctuation suggest about the guard who says this line?
2 In lines 3–5, what is going to stay the same, and what will be different?
3 The two sides are divided by a 'thick iron chain'. Why do you think the writer uses the words 'thick' and 'iron'?
4 'The border guards told her off.' Look for all the mentions of the guards in the poem.
   a How is the reader invited to think of them?
   b What does this make you think about the authorities behind the guards?
5 In the fourth **stanza** the mother is speaking to the children.
   a How does the writer make this sound like speech to a child?
   b Do you think she believes what she says?
6 What does the child conclude from comparing the two sides of the border?
7 It is autumn, and it is raining on both sides of the border. Apart from being a literal description, how might these two details reflect the situation?
8 The man 'kissed his muddy homeland'. Again, what can 'muddy' reflect other than the mud itself?
9 Who are 'all of us', do you think?

Words/phrases to explore (AO1 and AO2)

Activity 2

'The same chain of mountains encompassed all of us.' This is the fourth time in the poem that the word 'chain' is used. The implications of 'chain' seem very different here from the 'thick iron chain'.
1 Could they be the same in any way?
2 How might both sides still be 'chained'?

Comparing poems

Activity 3

1 **Comparing ideas and themes**
   Compare how individual people caught up in war are shown in 'At the Border' and 'Bayonet Charge'.
2 **Comparing writers' devices**
   Compare the effects of the chain in 'At the Border' and the leaves in 'The Falling Leaves'.

GradeStudio

Sample answer A

To achieve an A on this AO2 descriptor, you need to show **exploration of ideas/themes**. The following extract from a sample answer would hit the grade A requirement.

The message of the poem seems simple enough, that both sides of the border are the same, meaning that the boundary is artificial, like the chain that divides the two sides. 'The same chain of mountains encompassed all of us' suggests that divisions are false. Perhaps, though, 'chain' also implies that both sides are subjugated, not free, as the tone of the poem seems to suggest.

▶ Poem Glossary

Belfast Confetti during the troubles in Northern Ireland, the isolated Catholic area in the Short Strand was often pelted with objects such as those listed in line 2, which were thrown over the barriers into the houses. This became known as Belfast confetti, and was sometimes placed inside bombs, becoming shrapnel

Balaclava…Street streets in Belfast, but also the names of famous battles

Saracen, Kremlin 2-mesh the items in this line were all used by British soldiers on the streets; Saracens are armoured personnel carriers

Belfast Confetti

by Ciaran Carson

Read the poem in your AQA Anthology, then complete the activities below.

Initial responses

Activity 1

1 What is ironic about the term 'Belfast confetti'? Think what confetti is usually associated with, and what is happening in the poem.

2 To get into this poem, imagine a writer in the battle area trying to write. Punctuation marks are **metaphors** for the events and feelings that occur.
   a Why do you think the objects listed in line 2 are described as 'exclamation marks'?
   b Why is the explosion 'an asterisk on the map'?
   c Why is the burst of rapid fire like a 'hyphenated line'?
   d Why do you think the sentence 'kept stuttering'? Try to think of more than one reason.

3 From lines 5–7, what do you think the **speaker** is trying to do and what is he feeling about his situation? Base your ideas on details in the text.

4 Line 8 details items used by the riot squad. Why do you think the writer presents them like this? How does it make them appear to the reader? What does it reveal about the attitude of the city's inhabitants?

5 Look at the last line.
   a The speaker is challenged on the street. Why is this described as 'a fusillade of question marks'?
   b What else is being questioned here by the speaker? Why is the speaker questioning these things?

Words/phrases to explore (AO1 and AO2)

Activity 2

'Dead end again.' Explore what this means and implies in the poem. Think about the names of the streets the speaker is trapped in.

Comparing poems

Activity 3

1 **Comparing ideas and themes**
   Compare how individual people caught up in war are shown in 'Belfast Confetti' and 'Bayonet Charge'.

2 **Comparing writers' devices**
   Compare the ways in which **imagery** is used in 'Belfast Confetti' and 'Bayonet Charge'.

Poppies

by Jane Weir

Read the poem in your AQA Anthology, then complete the activities below.

Initial responses

Activity 1

1. In the first **stanza** the **speaker** is describing pinning a poppy onto her son's blazer. The clothing here is literal, but sometimes the writer uses **imagery** drawn from clothing, for example 'my stomach makes tucks, darts, pleats'. What feeling is the speaker conveying here? Find more examples of clothing imagery, and decide why they're used.

2. 'Spasms of paper red, disrupting a blockade' describes the poppy on the blazer, but the writer uses words that make the reader think of war or injury. Find other examples of this technique.

3. In the second stanza the speaker 'steeled the softening of her face'. Why do you think her face softens, and why does she 'steel' it?

4. She wants to play at being Eskimos like 'when you were little'. Find as many other references as you can to the son's childhood.

5. Why do you think the mother finds her words 'slowly melting'? What effect does the stanza break before this phrase have on the reader?

6. When the front door is opened, the world is 'overflowing like a treasure chest'. Whose point of view is this, do you think?

7. Look at the last stanza.
   a. 'The dove pulled freely against the sky'. What does the dove symbolise here, and how, exactly?
   b. The mother hopes to hear 'your playground voice catching on the wind'. What is the effect of the last line on the reader?

Words/phrases to explore (AO1 and AO2)

Activity 2

The writer describes herself leaning against the war memorial 'like a wishbone'. Find as many things to say about this comparison as you can.

Comparing poems

Activity 3

1. **Comparing ideas and themes**
   Compare the feelings shown by the speakers in 'Poppies' and 'At the Border'.

2. **Comparing writers' devices**
   Compare how feelings are shown in 'Poppies' and 'The Right Word'.

Futility

by Wilfred Owen

Read the poem in your AQA Anthology, then complete the activities below.

▶ **Poem Glossary**

fatuous idiotic, foolish

GradeStudio

Sample answer Ⓐ

To achieve an A* on this AO1 descriptor, you need to show **evaluation of the writers' uses of language and/or structure and/or form and their effect on readers**. To do this, you have to analyse detail and suggest its overall effect. The following extract from a sample answer would hit the grade A* requirement.

Activity 2

The idea that the sun might rouse the corpse is examined in the second stanza. It can wake seeds, and woke the planet, but here is helpless. All the sun's endeavour, and with it human life itself, is pointless if this is the outcome, as the final couplet makes clear – 'fatuous' seems to be spat out, just as the war has spat out this corpse onto the cold ground.

Initial responses

Activity 1

1 a What was the occupation of the soldier in peace time?
b Why is this significant in the poem?
2 At the end of the first **stanza**, the sun is described as 'kind'. What other words in this stanza suggest that the sun is 'kind'?
3 The other adjective about the sun in that line is 'old'. How is the idea of the sun being 'old' used at the beginning of the second stanza?
4 How does Owen make the death of the soldier seem more important than just a single death in the second stanza?
5 There are three questions in the second stanza. Why does Owen choose to use questions here?
6 What is the effect of the dashes in the line beginning 'Full-nerved'?
7 The man's sides are 'still warm'. How do ideas about warmth and cold occur all the way through the poem?
8 a What do you think the line beginning 'Was it for this' means?
b Where has the idea of 'clay' occurred before, and how does this connect with the death of the soldier?
9 What do you think the **tone** of the last two lines is, and how is it created?
10 The poem is written in **half-rhyme** rather than full rhyme, as in 'seeds/sides': the consonants are the same, but the vowels change. Why do you think Owen chose this **form** for this subject?

Words/phrases to explore (AO1 and AO2)

Activity 2

The last line is about breaking sleep.
1 How is this idea used elsewhere in the poem?
2 How is it a suitable ending?

Comparing poems

Activity 3

1 **Comparing ideas and themes**
Compare the attitudes to death in war in 'Futility' and 'The Falling Leaves'.
2 **Comparing writers' devices**
Compare the effects of the writer's choices in the endings of 'Futility' and 'The Falling Leaves'.

The Charge of the Light Brigade

by Alfred, Lord Tennyson

Read the poem in your AQA Anthology, then complete the activities below.

Initial responses

Activity 1

1 How does Tennyson establish the feeling of the charge in the first two lines?
2 Four of the first five **stanzas** start with repeated words and phrases, but the second does not. What might the reader notice here that is not mentioned anywhere else?
3 'Was there a man dismay'd?' suggests the courage of the soldiers. Where else in the poem can you find details that suggest courage?
4 In the third stanza, how is it made clear that the men are surrounded?
5 Also in the third stanza there are two examples of **personification**. Find them, and decide why Tennyson used them – what effect do they have?
6 The word 'not' is repeated at the end of the penultimate line and the beginning of the last line of the fourth stanza. This is the only time in the poem that Tennyson does this. Why do you think he does it here?
7 How does the fifth stanza show the soldiers are returning?
8 Which words in the last stanza show the attitude that the poet thinks should be held?

Words/phrases to explore (A01 and A02)

Activity 2

'O the wild charge they made!' What are the meaning and **tone** of this exclamation? Think of more than one meaning of 'wild'.

Comparing poems

Activity 3

1 **Comparing ideas and themes**
  Compare the attitudes to death in battle in 'The Charge of the Light Brigade' and 'Futility'.
2 **Comparing writers' devices**
  Compare the ways in which battle is shown in 'The Charge of the Light Brigade' and 'Bayonet Charge'.

GradeStudio

Context

The charge took place at the Battle of Balaclava in 1854 against Russian forces. Due to mistakes in communication, over 600 cavalry charged into a valley with artillery. Nearly half of them were killed or wounded.

GradeStudio

Sample answer Ⓐ

To achieve an A on this AO1 descriptor, you need to show **analytical use of detail to support interpretation**. To do this, you need to look closely at some supporting detail. The following extract from a sample answer would hit the grade A requirement.

Activity 1, question 6
The repetition of 'not' across the last two lines of the fourth stanza shows the constant undercurrent of loss in the poem, emphasised by the position of the second at the beginning of a line. 'Not' has already been highlighted by its repetition in the same position in two consecutive lines in the second stanza.

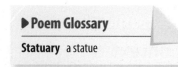

Bayonet Charge

by Ted Hughes

Read the poem in your AQA Anthology, then complete the activities below.

Initial responses
Activity 1

1 'Suddenly' sets off the active **tone** of the whole poem. Beginning with 'running', find as many words of action in the poem as you can. Notice how many present participles there are (words ending in '-ing', like 'running').

2 Hughes uses the senses a lot in this poem – seeing, hearing, smelling, tasting, touching. Beginning with 'raw', find as many examples as you can of the senses being used. What overall effect does this create for the reader?

3 A lot of the **imagery** in the poem is violent, such as 'smacking the belly out of the air'. Find some more examples, and think what effect each of them has – more than one effect, if you can.

4 What happened to the patriotic emotion that he was feeling before the action? Find evidence in the poem.

5 The soldier almost stops in the second **stanza**. Why is he bewildered? Again, find evidence.

6 Although there is a pause in the action, Hughes still makes the second stanza seem active. How does he do this?

7 a What seems nightmarish about the 'yellow hare'?
  b What else in the poem seems to belong to a nightmare?
  c Why do you think Hughes wants this effect?

8 Look at the list of the things 'dropped' by the soldier towards the end of the poem. How does the writer make these things seem both important and unimportant?

Words/phrases to explore (A01 and A02)
Activity 2

Having worked through the whole poem:
1 How do each of the last three words relate to the rest of it?
2 Why is 'dynamite' an effective last word?

Comparing poems
Activity 3

1 **Comparing ideas and themes**
Compare the attitudes to patriotism in 'Bayonet Charge' and 'next to of course god america'.

2 **Comparing writers' devices**
Compare the presentation of violence in 'Bayonet Charge' and 'Belfast Confetti'.

GradeStudio

Sample answer A*

To achieve an A* on this AO1 descriptor, you need to show **evaluation of the writers' uses of language and/or structure and/or form and their effect on readers**. To do this, you have to look carefully at a writer's choice. The following extract from a sample answer would hit the grade A* requirement.

Activity 1, question 8

The list in line 20 is very carefully organised: 'human dignity' seems much more basic than the high-sounding 'King' and 'honour', and undercuts the effect, but 'etcetera' at the end suggests they are all lost in the panic, or 'Dropped', placed sharply at the beginning of the next line.

The Falling Leaves
by Margaret Postgate Cole

Read the poem in your AQA Anthology, then complete the activities below.

▶ **Poem Glossary**

Flemish many of the 1915 battles of the First World War, such as Ypres, were fought in the Flemish areas of Belgium

Initial responses

Activity 1

1 The last line of the poem establishes that the dead soldiers are being compared to snowflakes.
  a What else are the soldiers compared to in the poem?
  b Why do you think Cole compares them to these things?
2 The leaves – and the soldiers – are described as 'brown' in the second line. Why?
3 Why does Cole choose a 'still' afternoon? Think of more than one reason.
4 The flakes fall 'thickly, silently'. What do these words suggest about what is going on, and what feelings do they create?
5 The deaths of the soldiers are 'wiping out the noon'. Suggest as many reasons as you can for the writer's choice of these words. Think about the day, and the soldiers.
6 Who are the 'gallant multitude' in line 8?
7 a Why do you think Cole describes the soldiers' 'beauty'? What is this 'beauty' compared to, do you think?
  b Is this just physical beauty?

Words/phrases to explore (AO1 and AO2)

Activity 2

The last word of the poem is 'clay', forming a full **rhyme** with 'lay', the only one in the poem.
1 How is this word something new in the poem?
2 Why is it effective because of its associations?
3 Why does the poet choose to use rhyme here and not elsewhere?

Comparing poems

Activity 3

1 Comparing ideas and themes
  Compare the attitudes to death in 'The Falling Leaves' and 'Futility'.
2 Comparing writers' devices
  Compare the ways in which the **tones** of the poems are created in 'The Falling Leaves' and 'The Charge of the Light Brigade'.

GradeStudio

Sample answer Ⓐ

To achieve an A* on this AO1 descriptor, you need to show **evaluation of the writers' uses of language and/or structure and/or form and their effect on readers**. To do this, you have to look carefully at a writer's choice. The following extract from a sample answer would hit the grade A* requirement.

> The alliteration of 'w' in line 4, combined with the actions of 'whirled' and 'whistling', catches the sound and movement of leaves caught in the wind; but these are soldiers, who seem to fall heavily and slowly, their fall slowed by the short line 5, with only three words and two commas.

Contexts

Austerlitz a famous battle in 1805 in the Napoleonic wars, though this poem is set at an unknown time in the future

Pan the Greek god of shepherds, who played pipes fashioned from reeds. He was a notorious seducer of nymphs. Kenneth Grahame refers to him in a chapter of *The Wind in the Willows* called 'The Piper at the Gates of Dawn'

▶ **Poem Glossary**

ominous suggesting that something unpleasant might happen

sentinel sentry

Sample answer Ⓐ

To achieve an A on this AO1 descriptor, you need to show **exploration of ideas/themes**. To do this, you have to explore several ideas in the text. The following extract from a sample answer would hit the grade A requirement.

> Death in the poem is seen as desirable, almost as a lover, but at the same time laden with grief. When the mind dies, the body follows, it seems; Vaudevue's memory is 'dead for evermore', and she is drawn straight to the icy waters of death.

Come On, Come Back
by Stevie Smith

Read the poem in your AQA Anthology, then complete the activities below.

Initial responses

Activity 1

1 Vaudevue's mind has been affected. How is this made clear in the first **stanza**?
2 How does the writing suggest that this event takes place in a future battle?
3 The movement of the poem is quite uneven in the first three stanzas, but lines 16–17 beginning 'The sand beneath' have a much livelier sound. Say them aloud to hear this. What makes them lively and even? Think about **rhythm** and **rhyme**, and how this is different from what has gone before.
4 The pace continues into the next stanza. How does Smith achieve this?
5 The lake is described as 'adorable'. How is it made to seem romantic in this stanza?
6 Why do you think Vaudevue might be attracted to the lake? Try to find two more examples of the lake being seen romantically.
7 Look at lines 22–27 beginning 'The waters'. What is the source of Vaudevue's grief, do you think?
8 Read the **context** at the top of this page about Pan. Why do you think Smith suggests that the enemy sentinel is like Pan?

Words/phrases to explore (AO1)

Activity 2

Having read and thought about the whole poem, think about the effects of the last line, which is also the title. Do we want Vaudevue to 'come back'?

Comparing poems

Activity 3

1 **Comparing ideas and themes**
Compare the experiences of death in 'Out of the Blue' and 'Come On, Come Back'.
2 **Comparing writers' devices**
Compare the ways in which an individual's experiences are shown in 'Come On, Come Back' and 'Bayonet Charge'.

next to of course god america

by e.e. cummings

Read the poem in your AQA Anthology, then complete the activities below.

Initial responses

1 Cummings uses **enjambment** in this poem. What effect does it have?
2 The **speaker** in the poem uses lines from various songs or poems, but doesn't quite complete them. 'The dawn's early –' should be completed with 'light'. (It is the opening line from 'The Star Spangled Banner'.)
   a Can you recognise any other incomplete lines?
   b What effect do these omissions have on the reader's impressions of what the speaker is saying?
3 The speaker seems to be trying to make a patriotic speech. Does 'and so forth' help his case? What effect does it have, do you think?
4 What impression does 'we should worry' create of American attitudes to history?
5 The speaker says that America's 'sons' acclaim its glory using expressions such as 'by gee'. Why doesn't this seem right?
6 The poem is a **sonnet**, with a regular **rhyme scheme**. Line 11 doesn't quite work, though, as the scheme breaks down on the word 'slaughter', and it is the first line where the word at the end doesn't lead on to the next line. The word 'slaughter' is therefore brought to the reader's attention.
   a How does this word affect what the previous two lines were saying?
   b What does it directly contrast with?
   c Why do you think it is described as 'roaring' slaughter? What sort of picture does this create?
7 Think about lines 12 and 13.
   a What sort of death did the 'heroic happy dead' die?
   b What is the obvious answer to the question in line 13, even if it's not what the speaker intended?

Words/phrases to explore (AO1)

Think about the effect of the last line.
1 Why is it there?
2 What is the writer's attitude to what the speaker says?
3 How do you know, exactly?

Comparing poems

1 **Comparing ideas and themes**
   Compare the attitudes to death in 'next to of course god america' and 'The Charge of the Light Brigade'.
2 **Comparing writers' devices**
   Compare the ways in which the writers attack the idea of patriotism in 'next to of course god america' and 'Flag'.

GradeStudio

Sample answer (A*)

To achieve an A* on this AO2 descriptor, you need to show **evaluation of the writers' uses of language and/or structure and/or form and their effect on readers**. To do this, you have to judge the final effect on the reader. The following extract from a sample answer would hit the grade A* requirement.

> Activity I, question 6
>
> 'Slaughter' brings the reader up sharply against the realities of the results of patriotism. The speaker's frantic attempts to convince have already been undercut by the truncated lines and the unfortunate implications of phrases like 'and so forth' and 'why should we worry', but now the truth is presented graphically. Forced by the word itself, which is in sharp contrast to the abstract ideas in the poem so far, and by the sudden change of rhyme to confront the word, the reader can only conclude that no 'beauty' is implied in the 'roaring' conflict. The deaths conjured are ugly as well as mindless.

Hawk Roosting

by *Ted Hughes*

Read the poem in your AQA Anthology, then complete the activities below.

▶ Poem Glossary

sophistry subtle reasoning or argument

GradeStudio

Sample answer Ⓐ

To achieve an A on this AO2 descriptor, you need to show **analysis of the writers' uses of language and/or structure and/or form and their effect on readers**. To do this, you have to look carefully at a writer's device. The following extract from a sample answer would hit the grade A requirement.

> In lines 3 and 9 of 'Hawk Roosting' the language is deliberately blunt. The alliteration of 'k' sounds in the repeated 'hooked', and then in 'locked' and 'bark', and in mostly monosyllabic words, seem as hard and sharp as the hawk itself.

Activity 1

Initial responses

1 The first word of the poem is 'I'.
   a Find and jot down all the examples you can find of 'I', 'me', or 'my' in the poem.
   b What does this tell you about the hawk?
2 'I hold Creation in my foot'. Find as many examples as you can of the hawk's feeling of power in the poem.
3 If the hawk were human, what sort of person would he be? Think about your responses to the first two questions.
4 **a** What does the hawk dream of?
   b What sort of dream would a 'falsifying dream' be, do you think? Think of the attitudes in some of the other poems you have read.
5 Why might the hawk think that nature was made for him? Look at the second **stanza**.
6 Look at the first line of the third stanza. How does the writer make the hawk seem strong here? Think about the length and sound of the words.
7 How does the language of the last line of the fourth stanza contrast with 'sophistry' in the previous line?
8 'No arguments assert my right:'. What does assert the hawk's right? Notice the effect of the colon at the end of this line.
9 Each of the lines in the last stanza is **end-stopped** – it has a full stop at the end, forming a single sentence. Why does the writer do this? What final impression does it leave of the hawk?

Activity 2

Words/phrases to explore (A01)

'Now I hold Creation in my foot'. How exactly is this true? Think of as many reasons as you can.

Activity 3

Comparing poems

1 **Comparing ideas and themes**
   Compare the characters created in 'Hawk Roosting' and 'Bayonet Charge'.
2 **Comparing writers' devices**
   Compare the ways in which the writers of 'Hawk Roosting' and 'The Falling Leaves' use language to create mood.

Looking at the poems individually: what have you learned?

My learning ▷

In this section you will:
- think about which poems interested you most and why.

Complete Activities 1 and 2 below. As you do, think about which poems and which features of poems were most interesting to you. If you're working with someone else, you could learn from each other, or consider what differences in choices might reveal about you as readers.

Note that the words in bold in the tasks below refer to the key words in the Assessment Objectives.

Assessment Objective 1 (AO1)

Activity 1

1 Which of these poems did you **respond** to most strongly? You may have liked it, or disliked it, or found it the most interesting, or horrible. You may have a number of things to say about it.

Working with a partner, or by yourself, display your responses as a spider diagram, and then compare it with someone else's, to see if you have responded to the poems in similar ways.

2 Which poems did you find it easiest to offer an **interpretation** about? In other words, you had a view about a poem's meaning that you could argue from the text and **select detail** to support your view. For instance, you might have found it easy to argue and support the view that 'The Charge of the Light Brigade' is a poem about bravery.

Suggesting more than one interpretation of a poem, or parts of a poem, gives you opportunities to score more marks. For instance, you could respond to the final stanza of 'The Yellow Palm' as either a life-giving moment or a moment of destruction.

Assessment Objective 2 (AO2)

Activity 2

1 Which features of **language**, **structure** or **form** did you understand best? The most promising ones to write about in the exam will be the ones where you have most to say. For instance, you might have found several things to say about:
- the effect of the repetitions at the end of 'Come On, Come Back' (language)
- the effects of language and stanza at the end of 'The Right Word' (structure)
- the effects of the half-rhymes in 'Futility' (form).

When answering this question, it would be best if you chose your own examples rather than using the ones above!

2 What **ideas** did you identify in the poems? Again, the best answers will probably identify several ideas in a poem, or several aspects of one idea. For instance, you might have identified or explored more than one idea about war in 'The Charge of the Light Brigade.'

My learning ▶

In this section you will learn how to:
- compare poems and address the Assessment Objectives
- develop writing skills and practise exam-style questions.

Comparing the 'Conflict' poems

Assessment Objective 3 is broken into two parts:

▶ comparing ideas and themes in the poems, with detail

▶ comparing the ways writers use language or structure or form, with detail.

In responding to the exam question, you will need to address both these parts.

Comparing ideas and themes

Read the poems 'Mametz Wood' and 'Futility', then complete the activities below.

Assessment Objective:

The Assessment Objective you will be focusing on in this part of the chapter is:

AO3 make comparisons and explain links between texts, evaluating writers' different ways of expressing meaning and achieving effects.

Activity 1

Focusing on ideas and themes in the two poems, list as many similarities and differences as you can. For example: both poems are about the deaths of soldiers in war; both poems refer to nature a lot; the poems take place at different times – one immediately after the death, one years later.

Activity 2

GradeStudio

Sample answer **B**

To achieve a B on this AO3 descriptor, you need to make a **developed comparison of ideas and/or meanings**. The following extract from a sample answer to the task in Activity 3 would hit the grade B requirement.

Using your lists of similarities and differences from Activity 1, decide how different the poems are for each point you made. For example, 'Futility' seems full of emotions about the death, but 'Mametz Wood' seems a lot more objective. What emotions can you find in 'Futility'? Can you find any of those emotions in 'Mametz Wood'? Are the emotions equally strong in both poems?

Use quotations or refer to the poem to support what you think.

Both poems have some suggestions of life being restored, but in different ways. The speaker in 'Futility' is hoping that the soldier can be roused by 'the kind old sun', because it has always woken him until this moment. This will not happen, though. In 'Mametz Wood' the soldiers died years ago, and the land itself is healing, so life will be restored in a way, though in both situations the soldiers have died.

'Futility' is much more emotional, which the word 'kind' shows, as the soldier has died so recently that it seems as if he might really breathe again. When he doesn't, pleading turns to anger.

'Mametz Wood' is much more impersonal: death happened a long time ago.

Find a detail from each poem that you could compare directly.
For example:

> as they tended the
> land back into itself

(Mametz Wood)

> If anything might rouse him now
> The kind old sun will know

(Futility)

Write two or three paragraphs exploring all the similarities and differences you can find, asking yourself:

- Which statement is more personal? Why?
- Which restoration is successful, and in what way?
- How is the outcome the same in each?
- How does each detail fit into the poem as a whole?

Comparing writers' methods

Now you need to think about the similarities and differences in terms of the methods the writers use, and why they use them. For these two poems, you could say:

 both use nature to describe death

 both personify nature – the earth in 'Mametz Wood' and the sun in 'Futility'.

 'Futility' uses half-rhyme, whereas 'Mametz Wood' doesn't rhyme at all until the last three lines.

These are fairly simple links, though, rather than comparisons which explore or analyse. Better marks can usually be achieved by taking two details or quotations which have some similarity and exploring them.

Look at:

- 'the blown/and broken bird's egg of a skull' (Mametz Wood)
- 'are sides/Full-nerved – still warm – too hard to stir?' (Futility).

Explore the similarities and differences between these details:

1 Which of these is a **metaphor**, and which is a literal description?
2 How does each one suggest that life is fragile?
3 One of these is a statement, but the other is a question. What difference does it make?
4 One of these lines is smooth and continuous, but the other is full of pauses. What do the writers use to create this, and what different effects do they have on the reader?

You should have found a lot of things to say, to form the basis of a detailed comparison. Making a good choice of details to write about, where you have plenty to say, is a key skill for the exam.

GradeStudio

Sample answer

To achieve an A* on this AO3 descriptor, you need to make an **evaluative comparison of writers' uses of language and/ or structure and/or form and their effects on readers, with detail** as this sample answer to the task in Activity 4 does.

> Life is fragile in both poems. The skull is not just like an egg, but a bird's egg, easily smashed, and 'blown' – the life has been sucked out of it. Similarly, the balance between life and death in 'Futility' seems very slight: the speaker seems to think that the nerves are still intact, and the blood warm, so the body could easily come to life. The difference is one of time: the body in 'Mametz Wood' is so old that it has decayed, whereas the body in 'Futility' is freshly dead. This accounts for the difference in tone: one is a simple, unbroken, impersonal observation, though the implied delicacy of the egg suggests a value placed on the life. The other is urgent and angry, the strength of the emotion conveyed through the dashes, and the effect of the comma and the line break after 'sides'.

Putting it all together

To practise the skills you've been working on in these comparison activities, here are two more activities on a different pair of poems: 'Bayonet Charge' and 'The Charge of the Light Brigade'.

1 What ideas and themes can you find in the poems which are similar? What attitudes to war can you find in the poems? What similarities and differences are there in the physical details about the soldiers' experiences in battle? What do they feel about what they are going through? List as many similarities and differences as you can.

2 Now you have a list of similarities and differences between the two poems, you can consider how similar they are, or how different. For instance, there is a lot of movement in both poems, but is it the same sort of movement? How does it differ? Include some detail or evidence to support each point.

3 Find a detail from each poem that you could compare directly, for example:

> Flash'd all their sabres bare
> Flash'd as they turned in air

(The Charge of the Light Brigade)

> He lugged a rifle numb
> as a smashed arm

(Bayonet Charge)

The simple link between the two details is that they both describe the soldiers' weapons, but to reach the grades you are aiming for, you need to explore all the similarities and differences you can find between the details.

So here you would need to consider:
- What difference does the type of weapon make?
- How are the senses used differently?
- What different attitudes are suggested by the descriptions?
- How does each detail fit into the poems as a whole in what they reveal about the **speakers**?

Once you have chosen your two details, write two paragraphs comparing them.

GradeStudio

Sample answer A

To achieve an A on this AO3 descriptor, you need to make an **analytical comparison of ideas and/or meanings and/or techniques**. The following extract from a sample answer to task 3 in Activity 5 would hit the grade A requirement.

> The soldiers in both poems are carrying weapons, but the effects are quite different. The rifle seems to weigh down the soldier in 'Bayonet Charge', as it is 'lugged', whereas the sabres are held up 'in air', almost as if they are lifting their carriers up, not weighing them down. 'Flash'd' suggests something bright and, in the context of the poem, uplifting and perhaps glorious, but the rifle is compared to a 'smashed arm', a depressing idea, with nothing glorious about it. The sabres 'turn'd in air', full of life, whereas the rifle is 'numb'.

Comparing writers' methods and purposes
Activity 6

Compare how the two writers finish the poems in the last four lines of each, exploring similarities and differences. Discuss or make notes on:

- the different attitudes to the word 'honour', and how the attitudes are conveyed
- the different feelings expressed in each, and how they are conveyed
- the differences in **rhyme** and punctuation between the two, and the effects they have.

GradeStudio

Sample answer B

To achieve a B on this AO3 descriptor, you need to make a **developed comparison of ideas and/or meanings and/or techniques**. The following extract from a sample answer to the task in Activity 6 would hit the grade B requirement.

> 'Honour' is an element in the ending of both poems, and in both is linked with nobility. 'King' is the first thing in the list in 'Bayonet Charge', and in 'Light Brigade' it is the soldiers themselves who are 'noble'. In 'Light Brigade', honour is a central idea, emphasised by its repetition at the beginning of succeeding lines, whereas in 'Bayonet Charge' it is only the second in a list, and only mentioned once. The list is to be 'dropped', though, because of the soldier's terror, whereas in 'Light Brigade' it is to be celebrated, which is emphasised by the exclamation marks at the end of the lines.

My learning

In this section you will learn how to:
- structure a response in the exam
- use the skills you have learned to perform successfully.

Assessment Objectives:

A01 respond to texts critically and imaginatively; select and evaluate relevant textual detail to illustrate and support interpretations.

A02 explain how language, structure and form contribute to writers' presentation of ideas, themes and settings.

A03 make comparisons and explain links between texts, evaluating writers' different ways of expressing meaning and achieving effects.

Writing in the exam

Writing your response – planning and structuring

In the exam you have to show the skills that you practised in the activities above. But how should you structure your writing to get the best marks that you can? Your process with any exam question should be: Read, Think, Write, Edit.

Read

Read the questions – what exactly are you being asked to do? The questions should remind you about the Assessment Objectives. There will be a choice of two questions, so you need to make a choice quickly. Each question will ask you to compare a named poem with an unnamed poem, so your choice might be based on the poem that is named, or on what each question is asking you to do.

Think

This is the planning stage. The first word of the exam task is likely to be 'compare'. One of the descriptors in the mark band for a grade B is 'sustained and developed comparison'. This suggests that a wise course of action would be to build your response around a comparison of the two poems.

This doesn't mean that everything you write should be comparative. Rather, you should think about and establish a comparative framework such as the one on page 88 before you write. Within that, you need to jot down quickly some of the ideas from the poems, and perhaps one or two details that you're planning to use – you should choose things that you can write quite a lot about.

The thinking is more important than the writing here. The whole process might take 5 minutes, perhaps (certainly not less than 2 minutes). You only have 45 minutes for the whole task. Don't start writing straight away, think about the question carefully first!

Write

When you write, what you are going to show is:

▶ what you think about the poems

▶ why they are written in the ways that they are

▶ what happens when you compare the poems, or parts of them.

In other words, these are the things the Assessment Objectives focus on. The last phrase, 'or parts of them', is important. No question will ask you to write down everything you know about the poems; you have to select from what you know to think and write about the poems in answer to this question, in the ways that you've practised as you've worked through this section.

Edit

If you have any time left, you should look for ways to improve your answer. Don't look for spelling or punctuation errors: these don't carry marks here. Could you quickly add another possible meaning of a word or phrase that you've written about? Is there another idea about the effect of a writer's choice of language? Additions of this kind might gain you an extra mark.

Putting it into practice

Let's take a typical exam question:

Compare (AO3) the ways in which the speakers' desperation (AO1) is presented in 'Out of the Blue' and one other poem from 'Conflict' (AO2).

Let's suppose that you chose 'Belfast Confetti' as a good poem to compare with 'Out of the Blue' – both show characters in similar difficult situations, feeling desperate, and the poems are written very differently.

First, you need to jot down a few ideas from the poems that you're going to use when you write. For example:

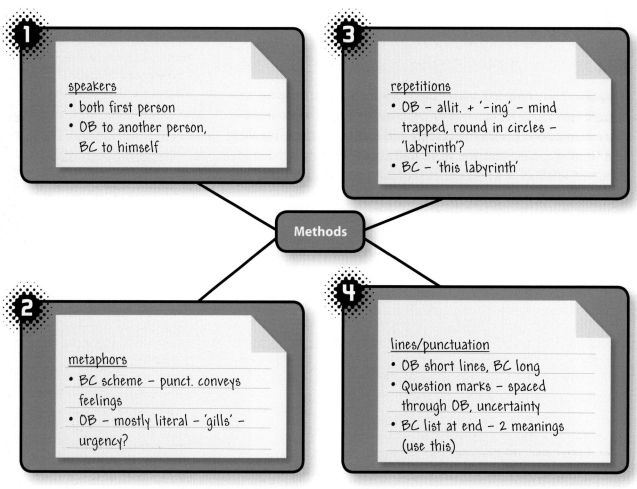

1
speakers
• both first person
• OB to another person, BC to himself

3
repetitions
• OB – allit. + '-ing' – mind trapped, round in circles – 'labyrinth'?
• BC – 'this labyrinth'

Methods

2
metaphors
• BC scheme – punct. conveys feelings
• OB – mostly literal – 'gills' – urgency?

4
lines/punctuation
• OB short lines, BC long
• Question marks – spaced through OB, uncertainty
• BC list at end – 2 meanings (use this)

In the notes above, the student decided that the desperation was similar, but the poems were different in method, so the response could be structured around different methods. Four ideas about method is plenty: the task is not to try to offer an exhaustive account – you are just showing off your thinking and writing skills.

After thinking of the four methods, the student jotted down some relevant notes, remembering that they all needed to be connected with 'desperation'. They then decided what order to write in (indicated by the numbers).

Read the extracts from these sample student answers, together with the question below and the examiner comments. You could then try the sample exam question at the end.

Compare the ways the speakers' desperation is presented in 'Out of the Blue' and one other poem from 'Conflict'.

Openings

B grade answer

Student A

The situations in these poems are very similar, in that the speaker is trapped, and in danger, and both speakers are certainly desperate. The poets' methods are very different, though. Both poems are written in the first person, but whereas 'Out of the Blue' is addressed to another person, 'you', 'Belfast Confetti' seems to be addressed only to himself. The speaker in 'Out of the Blue' is alone, and is desperately trying to be seen: 'Do you see me, my love?' In 'Belfast Confetti', the speaker has clearly been seen by the riot squad, and although alone, is questioned by them and is desperate to escape, as 'a fusillade of question marks' shows.

Examiner comment

Student A's response is already a **developed comparison of ideas and techniques** and is therefore already in the 18–24 mark band (equivalent to a grade B).

A grade answer

Student B

The situations in these poems are very similar, in that the speaker is trapped and in danger, and both speakers are certainly desperate. The poets' methods are very different, though. The first-person speaker in 'Out of the Blue' is desperate to be recognised properly for what he is, 'a soul worth saving'. The poem is dominated by 'I', 'me' and 'you', though it's a one-sided conversation. In 'Belfast Confetti' there is no 'you'. The first-person voice is alone, apart from the unwelcome attentions of the riot squad, but here there is speech with, or at least from, another person. The conversation is with himself, not the outside world, shown by the string of questions at the end – he desperately questions his own identity.

Examiner comment

Student B's response is a band stronger in terms of comparison, as it has **analytical use of detail** (25–30), and an **analytical comparison of ideas** and **language**. So it is already well into the 25–30 mark band (equivalent to a grade A).

Examiner comment

Both students get on with the task quickly, outlining the situation and starting to deal with and compare methods within the first two sentences. They don't start 'In this essay I am going to... ', which is usually a waste of time.

GradeStudio

A paragraph on a device

B grade answer

Student A

Both paragraphs use repetitions, but of different types. 'Out of the Blue' is full of language repetitions, through alliterations and participles, such as 'building, burning', or words, such as 'appalling. Apalling', which perhaps suggests a mind repeating itself, desperately going round in circles. Ciaran Carson describes this feeling, instead of conveying it through language repetition – the speaker tries to escape down different streets or alleyways, but 'can't escape'. He is in a 'labyrinth', which he can't get out of.

Examiner comment

In Student A's response, the first three sentences on 'Out of the Blue' hit the descriptor **analytical comparison of techniques** (25–30, equivalent to a grade A) very clearly, and it is followed with a developed comparison (18–24, equivalent to a grade B).

A* grade answer

Student B

Both paragraphs use repetitions, but to very different effect. 'Out of the Blue' is full of language repetitions, through alliterations and participles, such as 'building, burning', or words, such as 'appalling. Apalling', which perhaps suggests a mind repeating itself, going round in circles in desperation. 'Wheeling, spiralling, falling' captures this exactly: the words spiral, like the man's mind, and 'falling' describes his mental state and his rapidly approaching fate. Ciaran Carson describes this feeling, instead of conveying it through language repetition – the speaker tries to escape down different streets or alleyways, but 'can't escape'. He is in a 'labyrinth', which he can't get out of. Like the previous poem, 'labyrinth' describes his mental state as well as his physical situation: 'Where am I going?' is a cry which goes beyond the streets.

Examiner comment

Student B uses exactly the same ideas, but writes more about two details: 'spiralling' in 'Out of the Blue', and 'labyrinth' in 'Belfast Confetti'. In doing so, the response shows **evaluation of use of language** (31–36, equivalent to a grade A*) about 'spiralling' and **convincing interpretation** (31–36, equivalent to a grade A*) of 'labyrinth'as well as **analytical comparison of ideas** (25–30, equivalent to a grade A).

A paragraph on a detail

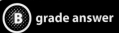 **grade answer**

Student A

Question marks run right through 'Out of the Blue', showing the speaker's uncertainty and desperation over what is happening to him. In 'Belfast Confetti' the questions are all in the last stanza – 'Why can't I escape?', followed by the three questions in the last line. These last questions suggest what the riot squad say when the speaker is challenged, 'a fusillade of question marks', but they also suggest the speaker doubting his own identity in this pressured situation, 'My name?'

Examiner comment

Student A finds two things to say about the effect of question marks in 'Belfast Confetti', hitting **appreciation of writers' use of language**, which is in the 18–24 mark band (equivalent to a grade B).

A* **grade answer**

Student B

Question marks run right through 'Out of the Blue', showing the speaker's uncertainty and desperation over what is happening to him. In 'Belfast Confetti' the questions are all in the last stanza – 'Why can't I escape?' followed by the three questions in the last line. Here the speaker's desperation takes on a new and unsettling dimension. While clearly echoing the riot squad's questioning, the writer omits to spell this out, allowing the reader to see the questions as internal as well. The speaker, stuck 'in my head', in the 'labyrinth' of his thoughts, questions who he is and why he is here – a deeper desperation in some ways than the man on the ledge, though his situation is physically terminal.

Examiner comment

Student B builds on this by finding more to say about the question marks, and achieving higher marks as a result. The sentence beginning 'While clearly' shows analysis of use of language (25–30, equivalent to a grade A), and this then moves both to **evaluation** and then **evaluative comparison** (31–36, equivalent to a grade A*) with the first poem.

You are now ready to tackle an exam question. Here's one to try:

Compare how attitudes to conflict are presented in 'Flag' and one other poem from 'Conflict'.

When you've written your answer, you could mark it, or get a partner to mark it, using the mark scheme on page 134.

My learning ▶

In this section you will learn how to:
- become familiar with the poems as a whole
- start to make links between the poems.

Getting to know the poems

Assessment Objectives:

AO1 respond to texts critically and imaginatively; select and evaluate relevant textual detail to illustrate and support interpretations.

AO2 explain how language, structure and form contribute to writers' presentation of ideas, themes and settings.

AO3 make comparisons and explain links between texts, evaluating writers' different ways of expressing meaning and achieving effects.

The poems

The Manhunt	**Brothers**	**To His Coy Mistress**
Simon Armitage	*Andrew Forster*	*Andrew Marvell*
Hour	**Praise Song for My Mother**	**The Farmer's Bride**
Carol Ann Duffy	*Grace Nichols*	*Charlotte Mew*
In Paris with You	**Harmonium**	**Sister Maude**
James Fenton	*Simon Armitage*	*Christina Rossetti*
Quickdraw	**Sonnet 116**	**Nettles**
Carol Ann Duffy	*William Shakespeare*	*Vernon Scannell*
Ghazal	**Sonnet 43**	**Born Yesterday**
Mimi Khalvati	*Elizabeth Barrett Browning*	*Philip Larkin*

The poems in this section are centred around different types of relationships between people. All the poems are in your AQA Anthology.

In this chapter you will be:

▶ looking at the individual poems

▶ comparing the poems

▶ learning how to approach exam questions.

As a result of this preparation you will be developing your writing skills in order to hit the Assessment Objectives. See page v for more information about what the Assessment Objectives mean. In the exam you will have to compare two poems from this chapter.

Getting started

The first thing to do is to start to familiarise yourself with the 'Relationships' poems. You can do the following activities by yourself, or in a group.

Activity 1

Read all the 'Relationships' poems in your AQA Anthology, quickly. Just notice what they seem to be about – don't worry about trying to make sense of every line.

Activity 2

Now find as many links as you can between some of the poems. You will need a large piece of paper with some headings on. Below is a list of ways you could look at the poems. You could use some of these to form your headings, though you could think of some of your own as well.

Ways to look at the poems	Tips on what to watch out for
What the poems are about	All the poems are about relationships – but what sort? There are different types of relationships here, and different feelings – attraction, uncertainty, anger, love, and so on. Which poems seem to have similar attitudes or types of relationship?
Beginnings/endings	Any similarities? How about lines that look a bit similar, but where there's a difference too? For example, both 'Hour' and 'The Farmer's Bride' use repetitions at the end. How are they similar or different in effect?
Length	You might notice some distinct similarities or differences. Include the number and length of **stanzas**, if there are any.
Rhyme	You need to look a little more carefully now. Is there a regular **rhyme scheme**? Does it change? What is the effect of **rhyme** in the poem? It's very different in 'Sonnet 43' and 'In Paris with You', for example.
Rhythm	Are there any poems with a strong **rhythm**, or a sudden change in rhythm? Look at the change at the end of 'To His Coy Mistress', for example. Are any of the others similar to this?
Language	Some of these poems make considerable use of repetition of words and phrases, but others hardly use repetition at all. Look for repetition in each poem. What effect does it have? If there is no repetition, why do you think the writer made that choice?
Imagery	Some poems are rich in **imagery**, such as **metaphors** and **similes**, while others might seem quite plain. Make a note of some obvious similarities and differences.

Now that you have found a lot of links, try displaying your findings in a different way, on a sheet of A3. Working on your own, in a pair or in a group, you could try any of the following ways.

1 Spread the titles out on the sheet and draw links between them, labelling each one.

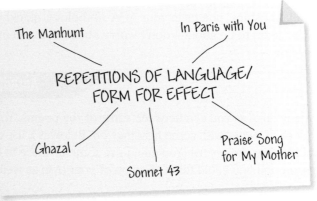

2 Draw a picture or symbol for each idea (such as death or nature) that appears in more than one poem, and group the poems around each – a poem can appear in more than one group.

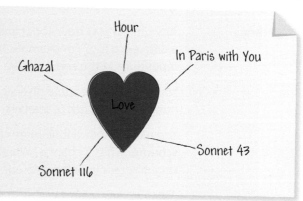

3 Draw a picture, or pictures, for each poem on the sheet, and link similar ones with arrows.

In these activities you have started to tackle all three Assessment Objectives. Now you will be focusing on AO1 and AO2 as you look at the poems individually (pages 95–111). You will return to AO3 when you compare the poems (pages 112–116). Finally, you will look at how to turn your knowledge and skills into successful exam answers, before you attempt one yourself (pages 117–121).

Looking at the poems individually

My learning ▶

In this section you will learn how to:
- develop your responses to the poems
- relate the Assessment Objectives to the poems.

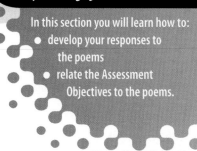

This section of the chapter, pages 95–111, is designed to lead you through an exploration of each individual poem. Throughout, you will find examples of student responses at different levels.

In the exam, you will have to write about the poems individually as well as comparing them.

In the exam you have to compare two poems; one named poem and one unnamed poem, which means you can choose the second one. On the Higher Tier paper the following will not be named poems: 'In Paris with You', 'Brothers', 'Sister Maude'. Of course, you could choose any of these poems to compare with the named one.

Assessment Objectives:

The Assessment Objectives you will be focusing on in this part of the chapter are:

 AO1 respond to texts critically and imaginatively; select and evaluate relevant textual detail to illustrate and support interpretations.

 AO2 explain how language, structure and form contribute to writers' presentation of ideas, themes and settings.

The Manhunt
by Simon Armitage

Read the poem in your AQA Anthology, then complete the activities below.

Initial responses

Activity 1

1 Read through the poem once, then trace the course of the bullet by picking out the body parts mentioned.

2 There are a lot of word patterns here.
   a Map the repetitions of 'only then'. When does the hunt move to the phase after 'only then'?
   b Pick out the verbs that describe what the **speaker** in the poem does. What picture do they give of her?
   c Trace the 'and…and' repetitions. When do they end? How do they add to the picture of what the speaker is doing?

3 Each part of the body (except one) is described with a **metaphor**. Find each one, and decide whether the metaphor is used to convey appearance, or some other quality.

4 The only part not to be described with a metaphor is the heart.
   a Why not?
   b The description of the heart is in the two shortest lines. Why does Armitage make this choice?

5 Why do you think the bullet is described as a 'foetus'?

6 What is the real source of the 'scarring', and why does the poet describe it as 'a sweating, unexploded mine'?

7 What does the speaker 'come close' to at the end, do you think?

Words/phrases to explore (AO1 and AO2)

Activity 2

1 Bearing in mind what you've found in working through the poem, what can you say about its title?

2 What different meanings can it have?

3 What sort of hunt is it?

Comparing with other poems

Activity 3

1 **Comparing ideas and themes**
   Compare the damage shown in 'The Manhunt' and 'Quickdraw'.

2 **Comparing writers' devices**
   Compare the ways in which the writers of 'The Manhunt' and 'Hour' use the same sort of metaphors throughout the poems.

Hour

by Carol Ann Duffy

Read the poem in your AQA Anthology,
then complete the activities below.

▶ **Poem Glossary**

Midas   in Greek myth, Midas
was a king who turned everything he
touched into gold

cuckoo spit   a froth left on plants
by insects

Initial responses   **Activity 1**

1   'Love's time's beggar' is Duffy's variation on
    'Love's not time's fool', which you can find in
    the Shakespeare **sonnet** on page 104. How is love
    'time's beggar'?

2   The phrase 'Love's time's beggar' sets up ideas about
    time and money. Pick out all the words about time and all
    the words about money in the poem.

3   A single hour 'makes love rich'. What things in the second **stanza**
    are described in terms of wealth?

4   'Flowers' and 'wine' are associated with things given to lovers,
    but these lovers prefer something simpler. In the first stanza, what
    simple things are as good as conventional lovers' gifts?

5   Find all the references to light in the poem. What sort of light
    is there?

6   The lovers seem to bribe ('backhanding') the night to come more
    slowly ('Time slows').
    a   How do they do this?
    b   What word implies that this takes a lot of doing?

7   Look at the last two lines. Why do you think Duffy isolates
    'Now' as a single word?

Words/phrases to explore (AO1 and AO2)   **Activity 2**

In the fairy tale 'Rumpelstiltskin', gold is spun from
straw.

1   How do the lovers spin gold from straw in
    the whole of this poem?

2   Why do you think Duffy repeats a word
    three times in the final line?

Comparing with other poems   **Activity 3**

1   **Comparing ideas and themes**
    Compare the ideas about time in
    'Hour' and 'To His Coy Mistress'.

2   **Comparing writers' devices**
    Compare the ways in which
    the writers present love in
    'Hour' and 'Ghazal'.

GradeStudio

Sample answer Ⓐ

To achieve an A on this AO2
descriptor, you need to show
exploration of ideas/themes.
The following extract from a
sample answer would hit the
grade A requirement.

> Time in the poem is
> seen as powerful – love
> has to beg from it – and
> malevolent, hating love,
> but it is also capable of
> being affected by the
> power of love: armed
> with the wealth of love,
> the 'millionaires' bribe it
> to move more slowly.

In Paris with You

by James Fenton

Read the poem in your AQA Anthology, then complete the activities below.

Initial responses
Activity 1

1 The **speaker** has had a bad experience in the past. Find all the clues you can in the first two **stanzas** to what has happened, and how he feels about it.

2 Although the speaker appears to be angry, the **tone** is quite light. How does Fenton achieve this? Look at the words he uses, and the **rhymes**.

3 Which word in the first stanza indicates that things might improve?

4 The poem sounds like somebody speaking. How does Fenton achieve this?

5 The fourth stanza has the shortest lines in the poem, which seems to slow the pace.
   a What does this suggest about the speaker?
   b What signs are there in this stanza that the speaker's wounds are healing?

6 The last stanza is full of repetitions.
   a Find all the repetitions.
   b What is the effect of the repetitions?

7 'Am I embarrassing you?' is the first question in the poem. Why do you think he uses one here? What does it show about the speaker?

Words/phrases to explore (AO1 and AO2)
Activity 2

Now that you've explored the whole poem, compare the last stanza with the first.
1 How has the speaker changed?
2 How does Fenton show the changes by the ways he writes the stanzas?

Comparing with other poems
Activity 3

1 **Comparing ideas and themes**
   Compare the attitudes of the speakers in 'In Paris with You' and 'To His Coy Mistress'.

2 **Comparing writers' devices**
   Compare the ways in which the writers use repetition in 'In Paris with You' and 'Praise Song for my Mother'.

GradeStudio

Sample answer B

To achieve a B on this AO1 descriptor, you need to show **details linked to interpretation**. The following extract from a sample answer would hit the grade B requirement.

> The speaker seems to wallow in his misery: 'tearful', 'resentful', and, tellingly, one of the 'talking wounded.' More evidence of this self-obsession is the fact that he rants to his partner throughout the poem, and only asks a question when he's clearly already in bed with her.

Quickdraw

by Carol Ann Duffy

Read the poem in your AQA Anthology,
then complete the activities below.

Initial responses

1 Look at the first word in the third line.
   a What is the effect of placing it exactly here?
   b Which word does it **rhyme** with?
2 **a** How might the voice be 'a pellet in my ear'?
   b What does that suggest about the state of the relationship?
3 What is the effect of space between the first two **stanzas**?
4 Look at the gunfighting **imagery** in the second stanza. Which of
   the fighters is more successful, and what do they succeed in doing?
5 The third stanza is full of images drawn from Westerns. What do
   they say about the state of the love affair?
6 Why is 'your kiss' described as 'silver bullets'? You may have to
   research what the phrase means.
7 What does each 'this' mean, and how can it have two meanings?

Words/phrases to explore (AO1 and AO2)

'You've wounded me' and 'through the heart' are both isolated on
the page.
1 Why does Duffy do this, do you think?
2 How are they the basis for the whole poem?

Comparing with other poems

1 **Comparing ideas and themes**
   Compare the relationships shown in 'Quickdraw' and 'In Paris
   with You'.
2 **Comparing writers' devices**
   Compare the ways in which the writers use **metaphors** in
   'Quickdraw' and 'Ghazal'.

GradeStudio

Context

The poem makes reference to
aspects of Westerns – Hollywood
films set in the American West.

GradeStudio

Sample answer Ⓑ

To achieve a B on this AO2
descriptor, you need to show
**appreciation/consideration of
writers' uses of language and/or
form and/or structure and their
effects on readers.** The following
extract from a sample answer
would hit the grade B requirement.

> **Activity 1, question 1a**
> The speaker's state of
> loneliness is stressed
> by placing 'alone' at the
> beginning of a line, after
> the slight pause that the
> line break gives. The full
> stop isolates it further.

Ghazal

by Mimi Khalvati

Read the poem in your AQA Anthology, then complete the activities below.

Initial responses

Activity 1

1 The **speaker** compares herself and her lover to a number of different types of things. In the first **stanza**, they are compared to 'the grass', 'the breeze', 'the rose' and 'the bird'. What type of things are these?

2 You can interpret what the speaker wants the lover to do in a number of ways. In the first stanza, 'woo me' is very clear. How do you think she is asking the lover to behave in the first line?

3 a What type of things does the speaker compare them to in the second stanza?
  b What is the effect of the **enjambment** here – the line break between 'hang' and 'on'?

4 The third and fourth stanzas revolve around 'tattoo me', using common tattoo **symbols**. What do you make of how the speaker would like the lover to behave here?

5 The fifth and sixth stanzas revolve around the idea of a tree. A 'laurel leaf' suggests that the speaker is a prize that the lover has won, but then the writer uses the tree idea in a different way, through 'bark'. Why would she like to be 'bark'? What does she want her lover to do?

6 'Marry' in the seventh stanza can mean 'match'. How would the speaker like the two of them to be matched? What different things would she like the lover to do?

7 How do the speaker's ideas get wider and larger in the last three stanzas? What does she compare herself and her lover to?

GradeStudio

Sample answer Ⓐ

To achieve an A* on this AO1 descriptor, you need to show **close analysis of detail to support interpretation**. The following extract from a sample answer would hit the grade A* requirement.

Activity 1, question 3

In the second stanza of the poem the writer uses the idea of poetry itself to explore the relationship. The simple idea is in the first line, with the lover being the 'rhyme', so being the leader, while 'I' is merely the refrain, following and repeating. The instruction not to 'hang', followed by 'come' suggests the speaker is really in control, though, and she will follow, 'come too', when the lover does as he is instructed by giving a 'cue'.

Words/phrases to explore (AO1)

Activity 2

Each second line is a **rhyme** with 'woo me'. Which of these seem definitely playful in effect, and which seem serious?

Comparing with other poems

Activity 3

1 **Comparing ideas and themes**
Compare the feelings of the speakers shown in 'Ghazal' and 'Sonnet 43'.

2 **Comparing writers' devices**
Compare the ways in which the writers present the feelings shown in 'Ghazal' and 'Sonnet 43'.

Brothers

by Andrew Forster

Read the poem in your AQA Anthology,
then complete the activities below.

Initial responses

Activity 1

1 How does the writer show what the **speaker's** attitude to his brother is in the first line? How does the writer emphasise this with the word order he has chosen?
2 In the first **stanza**, what don't the two older boys like about the young brother?
3 How is the attitude to the young brother shown again in the second stanza? How does the writer show that the two older boys feel superior?
4 What does the word 'windmilled' suggest about the young boy?
5 The idea of a race runs right through the third stanza.
   • How does the first line suggest that the two older boys are still children, really?
   • How does the third line make you think of a race, and perhaps of the 'Olympic Gold'?
   • The speaker 'ran on'. What was he running towards, and what was he running away from at the same time?
   • What 'distance' has the speaker 'set in motion' between himself and his brother, do you think?

Words/phrases to explore (AO1 and AO2)

Activity 2

'Unable to close the distance I'd set in motion'. How has the speaker's attitude changed from the first line of the poem? 'In motion' suggests something moving. What do you think this might imply about the relationship between the speaker and his brother after the time when this incident took place?

Comparing with other poems

Activity 3

1 **Comparing ideas and themes**
   Compare the feelings shown in 'Brothers' and 'Sister Maude'.
2 **Comparing writers' devices**
   Compare the ways that the writers present feelings in 'Brothers' and 'Sister Maude'.

GradeStudio

Sample answer **B**

To achieve a B on this AO1 descriptor, you need to show **details linked to interpretation**. The following extract from a sample answer would hit the grade B requirement.

> 'Grown-ups' are supposed to 'stroll the town', but the pace at the end tells of an older person's desperation about his relationship with his brother. He 'chased' and 'ran', but only towards failure. The 'hand' his brother reaches out does not reach him, and he is 'unable to close the distance' he has created.

Praise Song for My Mother

by Grace Nichols

Read the poem in your AQA Anthology, then complete the activities below.

Initial responses

Activity 1

1 Nichols uses natural **imagery** to describe her mother. How is she like water, and the moon, and sunrise?
2 This short poem is full of patterns. Look at the first three **stanzas**, and work out their repeated pattern. Why do you think she ends each one with a word ending '-ing'?
3 The stanza beginning at line 10 appears to break the pattern, but it's based on the same elements.
   a What things are the same? Think about threes.
   b Why do you think the final word is repeated this time?
   c What is the effect on the poem of breaking the pattern in this way?
4 The last line is the only separate line. Why do you think Nichols does this? What is the effect of the last line on the reader?
5 What is Nichols' attitude to her mother in the poem? Be as exact as you can.

GradeStudio

Sample answer Ⓐ

To achieve an A on this AO2 descriptor, you need to show **analysis of writers' uses of language and/or form and/or structure and their effects on readers**. The following extract from a sample answer would hit the grade A requirement.

Activity 1, question 2

In the third lines of the stanzas Nichols uses two adjectives first, with 'and', 'and' seeming to pile up the mother's qualities. Ending the lines with active words makes the mother seem active in her qualities, doubled again with 'replenishing' being repeated in the fourth stanza.

Words/phrases to explore (AO1 and AO2)

Activity 2

In this short poem, Nichols manages to include most of the elements (earth, air, fire and water) and the senses (sight, smell, touch, taste and hearing).
1 Find where these are referred to or suggested.
2 What is the effect of all of these together?

Comparing with other poems

Activity 3

1 **Comparing ideas and themes**
   Compare the feelings of the **speakers** in 'Praise Song for My Mother' and 'Sonnet 43'.
2 **Comparing writers' devices**
   Compare the ways in which the writers use repetition in 'Praise Song for My Mother' and 'Sonnet 43'.

Harmonium

by Simon Armitage

Read the poem in your AQA Anthology,
then complete the activities below.

Initial responses

1 The harmonium is 'gathering dust' and due to be 'bundled off to the skip'. Look through the poem for other references to things that are ageing or being disposed of.

2 How does Armitage **personify** (give human qualities to) the harmonium in lines 8 and 9?

3 The **speaker** can buy the harmonium 'for a song' and it 'struck a chord' with him.

   a How is the writer playing with words here?

   b What is it about the harmonium that attracts him? Look at the third **stanza** for a clue.

4 Look at the description of the speaker's father at the beginning of the last stanza. What is there here to remind you of the harmonium?

5 'we carry it flat, laid on its back.' How does this connect with what the father suggests in the following lines?

6 Look at the last six lines of the poem.

   a How does the speaker show that he knows himself and his father very well in these lines?

   b The idea of 'harmony' occurs a lot in this poem. How does the writer produce a 'harmony' between the two sentences in the last six lines?

   c How does the sound of the word 'him' in 'And he, being him' go with the ideas in the poem?

7 **a** In the whole poem, how does Armitage connect the harmonium with the speaker's father?

   b What does it reveal about his attitude to his father?

   c What effect does this have on the reader?

Words/phrases to explore (AO1 and AO2)

1 'too starved of breath to make itself heard.' Why can't he speak?

2 Now think of the way breath is used throughout the poem (a harmonium uses air, pushed by the action of the treadles, to play notes.) Why is it apt that the poem ends in silence?

Comparing with other poems

1 **Comparing ideas and themes**
   Compare the feelings about parents in 'Praise Song for My Mother' and 'Harmonium'.

2 **Comparing writers' devices**
   Compare the ways in which the writers show their feelings about their parents in 'Praise Song for My Mother' and 'Harmonium'.

▶ **Poem Glossary**

harmonium an organ with foot pedals (**treadles**)

Farrand Chapelette an old make of harmonium

beatify make sacred, make into saints

GradeStudio

Sample answer Ⓐ

To achieve an A on this AO2 descriptor, you need to show **exploratory response to text**. The following extract from a sample answer would hit the grade A requirement.

Activity 1, question 6b

The son has a number of attitudes to his father. Like the harmonium, he is ready to be 'bundled off to the skip', perhaps, as he is old and worn, and inclined to be maudlin, 'being him'. At the same time, he seems to admire his longevity and value the 'father and son' relationship, to the point where the actual idea of his death renders him speechless with grief.

GradeStudio

Sample answer **B**

To achieve a B on this AO1 descriptor, you need to show **considered/qualified response to text**. The following extract from a sample answer would hit the grade B requirement.

> The poem is full of definite statements about the unchangeable nature of love: it is 'never shaken', resistant to 'alteration', 'ever-fixéd.' But there is a moment of doubt: love's worth is 'unknown'.

Sonnet 116

by William Shakespeare

Read the poem in your AQA Anthology, then complete the activities below.

Initial responses

Activity 1

1 The poem offers a very definite view of love, something which is unchangeable. Which words in the first two lines make it definite?
2 'Love is not love' repeats the word 'love'. How does Shakespeare use the same technique in the following two lines?
3 'Ever-fixéd' suggests something that cannot be moved. How is this idea pictured in the following three lines?
4 How is love not the 'fool' of Time, do you think?
5 How does Shakespeare suggest in line 9 that young people are altered by time?
6 In lines 11 and 12, how is love made to seem everlasting?
7 The last two lines give a final, definite thought. How does Shakespeare make this thought seem both final and definite? Think about **form** here as well as meaning – the **rhyme** and the layout.

Words/phrases to explore (AO1 and AO2)

Activity 2

In the whole poem, how is love seen as an 'ever-fixéd mark'? Think about each part of this phrase, and how the ways Shakespeare writes reflects it.

Comparing with other poems

Activity 3

1 **Comparing ideas and themes**
   Compare the views about love shown in 'Sonnet 116' and 'Hour'.
2 **Comparing writers' devices**
   Compare the ways in which the writers present love in 'Sonnet 116' and 'Hour'.

Sonnet 43

by Elizabeth Barrett Browning

Read the poem in your AQA Anthology, then complete the activities below.

Initial responses

1 How many ways (of how the **speaker** loves 'thee') does the speaker give? Counting them will help to sort out the movement of the poem.

2 'the ends of Being and ideal Grace' describes a spiritual search. How does the whole sentence in lines 2–4 suggest something very large? Look at the way line 2 is written as well as what the words mean.

3 How do lines 5 and 6 suggest small things rather than large, but things for every time of day?

4 Look at the repetitions in lines 7–9. What effects do they have in conveying the speaker's feelings at this point? Try to be specific.

5 What has happened to the love that the speaker used to have for her 'lost saints'? Notice that she 'seemed' to lose it.

6 Look at the punctuation in lines 12 and 13. What effects do you think the dashes and the exclamation mark have? Remember that this is near to the end of her thoughts, too.

7 How is the final mention (of how the speaker loves 'thee') in some ways the biggest?

Words/phrases to explore (AO1 and AO2)

She will love him 'after death', 'if God choose'. This is a religious idea.

1 Where else in the poem does the poet use religious ideas? Look for words and phrases associated with religion.

2 What does this add to the poem, do you think?

Comparing with other poems

1 **Comparing ideas and themes**
   Compare the feelings about a loved one shown in 'Sonnet 43' and 'Hour'.

2 **Comparing writers' devices**
   Compare the ways in which love is shown in 'Sonnet 43' and 'Ghazal'.

GradeStudio

Sample answer Ⓐ

To achieve an A on this AO1 descriptor, you need to show **exploratory response to text**. The following extract from a sample answer would hit the grade A requirement.

> Barrett Browning seems to cover every possible part of life and thought in her determination to show her love. It is bigger than her soul's compass, so tiny it fills every corner of the day, and eminently noble – 'free' and 'pure'. It does seem to have replaced religious faith, though, which seems odd in one who seems to long for death, and the exclamation at lines 12 and 13 seems desperate. What is wrong?

To His Coy Mistress

by Andrew Marvell

Read the poem in your AQA Anthology, then complete the activities below.

GradeStudio

Sample answer Ⓐ

To achieve an A* on this AO1 descriptor, you need to show **close analysis of detail to support interpretation**. The following extract from a sample answer would hit the grade A* requirement.

> The third part of the argument is full of urgency from the beginning. Marvell both flatters (her skin is like 'morning dew') and urges his mistress, trying to persuade her that she is 'willing'. The fifth line is a direct exhortation, made powerful by every word being one syllable: 'Now' repeats the first strong word of the stanza, 'let' is the push, 'us' binds them together, 'while' stresses the short time available again, 'we' repeats the idea of the two joined, and 'may' is what he wants.

Initial responses

1 The three **stanzas** are like three stages of an argument. What are they? Look at the first line of each.
2 In the first stanza the **speaker** suggests what he and his mistress would do if they had all the world and endless time. Find all the references you can to places and stretches of time.
3 The speaker allots amounts of time to his mistress's body parts. Why do you think he leaves the heart till 'the last age'?
4 The attitude to time changes in the second stanza. Why do you think Marvell describes it as having a 'wingèd chariot'?
5 a Why does he describe eternity as a 'desert'? Remember what he is trying to achieve, and what deserts are like.
  b What other words and phrases in the second stanza suggest emptiness and death?
6 'Now' begins the third stanza. Look at the first seven lines, and find all the suggestions you can of 'now', and speed, youth and strength.
7 The eighth line is much slower.
  a How does Marvell make this line slower?
  b What is he describing, and why in this way?
8 The next four lines of the poem are very physical.
  a What is he describing?
  b What do you think he means by 'the iron gates of life'?

Words/phrases to explore (AO1 and AO2)

The last two lines complete the argument, but they also reflect it.
1 What is the speaker saying about time here?
2 How will the lovers 'make him run'?
3 How does the stanza stop (twice), then start again? Say the lines aloud, noticing how the stresses are different here from the lines in the rest of the poem.

Comparing with other poems

1 **Comparing ideas and themes**
  Compare the attitudes to another person in 'To His Coy Mistress' and 'Ghazal'.
2 **Comparing writers' devices**
  Compare the ways in which the writers use comparisons in 'To His Coy Mistress' and 'Ghazal'.

The Farmer's Bride

by Charlotte Mew

Read the poem in your AQA Anthology, then complete the
activities below.

Initial responses

1   What clues can you find in the first three lines to what goes wrong
    in the relationship?
2   The girl is described as running 'like a hare'.
    a   Find all the other comparisons you can between the girl and
        parts of nature, rather than 'all things human'.
    b   What evidence can you find that she is happier with animals
        than humans?
3   The last word of the second **stanza** is 'fast'. How is this given force
    by where it is placed, and by the punctuation?
4   What suggestion is made in the third stanza for the girl's preference
    for animals?
5   The short fourth stanza describes the girl from the point of view of
    the man. What does it reveal about his attitude to her?
6   The fifth stanza describes the time of year. How could some of
    these details relate to the story?
7   **a**   What do the repetitions in the last stanza reveal about the
        speaker's state of mind?
    b   How?
    c   What do you think is the effect of ending the story like this?

Words/phrases to explore
(AO1 and AO2)

'Alone, poor maid.' What is your
response to the girl's situation in
the poem? What difference does it
make that the story is narrated by
the husband?

Comparing with other poems

1   **Comparing ideas and themes**
    Compare the attitudes towards
    another person in 'The Farmer's
    Bride' and 'To His Coy Mistress'.
2   **Comparing writers' devices**
    Compare the ways in which the
    writers end the poems in 'The
    Farmer's Bride' and 'To His
    Coy Mistress'.

> ▶ **Poem Glossary**
>
> **fay**   a fairy or elf
> **leveret**   a young hare
> **rime**   frost

GradeStudio

Sample answer Ⓐ

To achieve an A* on this AO1
descriptor, you need to show
**evaluation of writers' uses of
language and/or form and/or
structure and their effects on
readers.** The following extract
from a sample answer would hit
the grade A* requirement.

Activity 1, question 6
The girl is strongly
associated with nature.
As the story draws to
its tragic conclusion,
the fifth stanza is full
of damage imagery:
tellingly, the bird's
feathers are torn, and
the black and white
make the reader think
of the main characters.
The ripening berries
are not comforting in
this context, and the
splash of red raises the
possibility of spilt blood.

Sister Maude

by Christina Rossetti

Read the poem in your AQA Anthology, then complete the activities below.

GradeStudio

Sample answer Ⓐ

To achieve an A* on this AO1 descriptor, you need to show **insightful exploratory response to text**. The following extract from a sample answer would hit the grade A* requirement.

> It is easy to sympathise with the speaker, who has been so betrayed by her sister, but we only hear her viewpoint. What exactly has she done? She describes her liaison with her 'dear' as 'my shame', placed at the beginning of her thoughts. Indeed, she can't get away from her own 'sin', whatever it is; the last word is 'sin', here below, where she remains. She is not sure of access to heaven. Why not? The reader is left with 'perhaps' about a lot of things at the end of the poem.

Initial responses
Activity 1

1 The **speaker** clearly dislikes Maude because of what she has done.
   a Which words in the first **stanza** suggest her dislike?
   b What things that she says in the rest of the poem suggest her dislike?
2 The second stanza shows the speaker's love of her 'dear'. How does Rossetti show her regret at his death by the way she writes the first line of the second stanza?
3 Her 'dear' is dead, and so is her father. The speaker's mother being 'at Heaven-gate' suggests she has recently died. How does this add to the effect of the poem?
4 The speaker hopes that Maude will stay with 'death and sin'.
   a What is she condemning her to?
   b Why these two things? Think about the whole poem.
5 What features does the poem have which make it seem a bit like a spell? Research spells, and then look for:
   a the threats and curses that the speaker makes
   b the way the writer uses repetitions of words, phrases and sentence forms
   c the way the writer uses **rhymes**.

Words/phrases to explore (AO1)
Activity 2

The last word of the poem is 'sin'.
1 What 'sins' are there in the poem, and where do they lead?
2 Is Maude the only sinner, do you think?

Comparing with other poems
Activity 3

1 **Comparing ideas and themes**
   Compare the state of mind of the speakers in 'In Paris with You' and 'Sister Maude'.
2 **Comparing writers' devices**
   Compare the ways in which the writers use repetition in 'Sister Maude' and 'In Paris with You'.

Nettles

by Vernon Scannell

Read the poem in your AQA Anthology, then complete the activities below.

Initial responses

1 The opening line is a simple statement. Find the other sentence which is like this one, and then decide why Scannell places them where he does.
2 Why does 'bed' seem to be a curious name for the place where the nettles grow?
3 'Regiment' is the beginning of an extended **metaphor** comparing the nettles to an army.
   a Find all the other military terms in the poem.
   b Why is the use of military terms apt here?
4 A metaphor like this is a way of conveying the **speaker's** emotions. Which word in line 3 does this more directly?
5 Why do you think the boy's grin is described as 'watery'?
6 'Not a nettle in that fierce parade/Stood upright'.
   a Which are the military words here?
   b Why 'fierce'?
7 What are the 'recruits' that have been called up? 'Sun and rain' just seems to describe weather. How could you describe them in a general term?
8 What emotions does the father have in this poem? Suggest more than one.

Words/phrases to explore (AO1 and AO2)

'My son would often feel sharp wounds again' is very general, compared to the specific first line.
1 How does 'wounds' continue the metaphor?
2 What 'sharp wounds' might the son feel, apart from nettle stings?
3 What does this reveal about the father's feelings and attitudes?

Comparing with other poems

1 **Comparing ideas and themes**
   Compare the attitudes towards a child in 'Nettles' and 'Born Yesterday'.
2 **Comparing writers' devices**
   Compare the ways in which the writers use metaphors in 'Nettles' and 'Quickdraw'.

▶ **Poem Glossary**

billhook a gardening tool with a hooked blade

honed sharpened

pyre a fire built to burn a body as part of a funeral

GradeStudio

Sample answer Ⓐ

To achieve an A on this AO1 descriptor, you need to show **analytical use of detail to support interpretation**. The following extract from a sample answer would hit the grade A requirement.

> The end of the story suggests that pain is inevitable. No sooner is a sacrifice offered to stop it than nature, in the form of 'sun and rain' grows the potential for fresh pain. This is a powerful force indeed, and the father knows it: the last line is definite, like the opening: the 'wounds' are unavoidable in life.

Born Yesterday

by Philip Larkin

Read the poem in your
AQA Anthology,
then complete the
activities below.

▶ **Poem Glossary**

Born Yesterday the saying
'I wasn't born yesterday' means 'I'm not
an innocent fool'

GradeStudio

Sample answer

To achieve an A* on this AO2
descriptor, you need to show
**evaluation of writers' uses of
language and/or form and/or
structure and their effects on
readers**. The following extract
from a sample answer would hit
the grade A* requirement.

> After the suddenly
> surprising list of
> distinctly adult
> qualities in lines 21–23,
> 'enthralled' hits a new
> note, emotional and
> almost magical, which
> leads to the almost
> conventional 'happiness'
> in the last line, but in a
> very unconventional way.
> The rhyme, its effect
> doubled by being the
> only one in the poem,
> serves to emphasise
> 'enthralled'. Perhaps the
> speaker is letting his
> emotions show through,
> despite himself.

Initial responses

1 In what ways is the baby like a 'tightly folded bud'? Think of all the
   implications the words have.
2 What is 'the usual stuff' that people wish for a baby, according to
   the **speaker**?
3 Find the first wish that the speaker makes for the child.
   a How is it phrased like a wish? Notice where it comes in the
     poem.
   b Why has the writer made this choice, do you think?
4 How might unusual talents adversely affect the child, according to
   the speaker?
5 Wishing for a child to be 'ordinary' and 'dull' may seem unusual, but
   look at the qualities the speaker wishes for the child in lines 21–23.
   What sort of qualities are these? How are these words different
   from words like 'innocence', 'love', 'ugly', 'good-looking'?
6 a Which word in the list is not downbeat like the rest of the poem?
   b How is the **tone** it suggests carried into the final line?
   c What is the effect on the reader of finishing the poem like this?

Words/phrases to explore (AO1 and AO2)

The title is 'Born Yesterday'.
1 How does this have two meanings?
2 How does this set the ideas for the whole of the poem? Think of as
   many reasons as you can.

Comparing with other poems

1 **Comparing ideas and themes**
   Compare the attitudes towards another person in 'Born Yesterday'
   and 'Praise Song for My Mother'.
2 **Comparing writers' devices**
   Compare the ways in which the writers present their views in 'Born
   Yesterday' and 'Praise Song for My Mother'.

Looking at the poems individually: what have you learned?

My learning ▶

In this section you will:
- think about which poems interested you most and why.

Complete Activities 1 and 2 below. As you do, think about which poems and which features of poems were most interesting to you. If you're working with someone else, you could learn from each other, or consider what differences in choices might reveal about you as a reader.

Note that the words in bold in the tasks below refer to the key words in the Assessment Objectives.

Assessment Objective 1 (AO1)

Activity 1

1 Which of these poems did you **respond** to most strongly? You may have liked it, or disliked it, or found it the most interesting, or horrible. It might mean that you had a number of things to say about it.
   Working with a partner, or by yourself, display your responses as a spider diagram, and then compare it with someone else's, to see if you have responded to the poems in similar ways.

2 Which poems did you find it easiest to offer an **interpretation** about? In other words, you had a view about a poem's meaning that you could argue from the text and **select detail** to support your view. For instance, you might have found it easy to argue and support the view that the speaker in 'Praise Song for My Mother' admires her mother.
   Suggesting more than one interpretation of a poem, or parts of a poem, gives you opportunities to score more marks. For instance, there are several ways you could interpret the nature of the speaker in 'The Farmer's Bride'.

Assessment Objective 2 (AO2)

Activity 2

1 Which features of **language**, **structure** or **form** did you understand best? The most promising ones to write about in the examination will be the ones where you have most to say. For instance, you might have found several things to say about:
   - the effect of the heart not being presented through a metaphor in 'The Manhunt' (language)
   - the gradual change in attitude in 'In Paris with You' (structure)
   - the effects of the spaces between stanzas in 'Quickdraw' (form).
   When answering this question, it would be best if you chose your own examples rather than using the ones above!

2 What **ideas** did you identify in the poems? Again, the best answers will probably identify several ideas in a poem, or several aspects of one idea. For instance, you might have identified or explored more than one idea about life in 'To His Coy Mistress'.

In this section you will learn how to:
- compare poems and address the Assessment Objectives
- develop writing skills and practise exam-style questions.

Comparing the 'Relationships' poems

Assessment Objective 3 is broken into two parts:

▶ comparing ideas and themes in the poems, with detail

▶ comparing the ways writers use language or structure or form, with detail.

In responding to the exam question, you will need to address both of these parts.

Assessment Objective:

The Assessment Objective you will be focusing on in this part of the chapter is:

AO3 make comparisons and explain links between texts, evaluating writers' different ways of expressing meaning and achieving effects.

Comparing ideas and themes

Read 'Sonnet 116' and 'Sonnet 43', then complete the activities below.

Activity 1

Thinking about ideas and themes in the two poems, list as many similarities and differences as you can. For example: both poems are about love.

Activity 2

Using your lists of similarities and differences from Activity 1, decide how different the poems are for each point you made. For example, 'Sonnet 43' seems full of personal emotions, but 'Sonnet 116' seems a lot more objective.

Use quotations or refer to the poem to support what you think.

Grade**Studio**

Sample answer **B**

To achieve a B on this AO3 descriptor, you need to make a **developed comparison of ideas and meanings**. The following extract from a sample answer to Activity 3 would hit the grade B requirement.

> Both poems suggest that love is something that cannot be changed. Indeed, Shakespeare makes just this point in several ways: love cannot be altered, bent or shaken, according to the first six lines. It is not changed by 'Time', even though the lovers may physically change. The 'height' of love suggests its size, which is also mentioned in the second line of 'Sonnet 43'. This poem has a number of ideas about the nature of love, not just one: it belongs in the life of the 'soul', of the mind, of daily life and passion, and seems both exalted and simple, 'with my childhood's faith'. Both poems end in a similar way, though, with the idea that love will last beyond life: 'to the edge of doom' (Shakespeare), and 'after death' (Barrett Browning).

Find a detail from each poem that you could compare directly. For example:

> O no! It is an ever-fixéd mark,
>   That looks on tempests and is never shaken
>
> (Sonnet 116)

> I love thee to the level of everyday's
>   Most quiet need, by sun and candle-light.
>
> (Sonnet 43)

Write two or three paragraphs exploring all the similarities and differences you can find, asking yourself:
- Which statement is more personal? How?
- Which one is literal, and which uses **imagery**?
- How is nature used in each?
- How does each detail fit into the poem as a whole?

Comparing writers' methods

Now you need to think about the similarities and differences in terms of the methods the writers use, and why they use them. For these two poems, you could say:

▶ both poems are written in 14 lines

▶ both poems have regular (but different) rhyme schemes

▶ Shakespeare uses imagery to describe the nature of love, whereas Barrett Browning's poem is written much more plainly.

These are fairly simple links, though, rather than comparisons which explore or analyse.

Better marks can usually be achieved by taking two details or quotations which have some similarity and exploring them.

Look at:

> O no! It is an ever-fixéd mark
>
> (Sonnet 116)

> I love thee with the breath,
> Smiles, tears of all my life!
>
> (Sonnet 43)

Explore the similarities and differences between these details:
- Which of these is a **metaphor**, and which is a literal description?
- What does each one suggest about love?
- Both of these lines use an exclamation mark. How are the effects different?
- Which of these is more personal? How?

You should have found a lot of things to say, to form the basis of a detailed comparison. Making a good choice of details to write about, where you have plenty to say, is a key skill for the exam.

GradeStudio

Sample answer A

To achieve an A* on this AO3 descriptor, you need to make an **evaluative comparison of ideas, meanings and techniques**. The following extract from a sample answer to Activity 4 would hit the grade A* requirement.

> Both poets make use of exclamation marks in the poems, but the effects could hardly be more different. Shakespeare's comes at the beginning of a line, and after 'O no'. It is the sort of measured exclamation that is made in the course of an argument, which is of course what this poem resembles, from the opening proposition, which is then unfolded in a number of ways, to the final couplet, which is almost legalistically phrased. There is nothing measured about the Barrett Browning poem. Although this poem is much more personal than Shakespeare's, the speaker addressing her lover directly rather than theorising, the rhythm is nevertheless measured until this moment. Now, however, with the dashes either side of the sentence spread across the centres of two lines, this sentence breaks the careful counting with an almost desperate outburst. This shows a strength of emotion that Shakespeare never tries to reach.

Putting it all together

To practise the skills you've been working on in these activities, here are two more activities on a different pair of poems: 'Hour' and 'Quickdraw'.

Activity 5

1   What ideas and themes can you find in the poems which are similar? For example, both poems are about love between two people.
    a   What differences in attitudes to the other person can you find in the poems?
    b   What similarities and differences are there in the effects of love on the **speaker**?
    c   What different feelings are shown?
        Think of as many similarities and differences as you can.
2   Now you've got a list of similarities and differences between the two poems, you can consider how similar they are, or how different. Can you find any common feeling between the two? How strong is it in each? Include some detail or evidence to support each point.

3 Find a detail from each poem that you could compare directly, for example:

> your voice
> A pellet in my ear

(Quickdraw)

> We are millionaires,
> backhanding the night

(Hour)

The simple link between the two details is that they both describe two people in a close relationship, but to reach the grades you are aiming for, you need to explore all the similarities and differences you can find between the details. So here you would need to consider:

- What different attitudes are revealed in the details?
- What is revealed about the nature of the relationship in each?
- How are the relationships shown in the details, and how are the relationships different?
- How does each detail fit into the poems as a whole, in what they reveal about the **speakers**?

Once you have chosen your two details, write two paragraphs comparing them.

GradeStudio

Sample answer A

To achieve an A on this AO3 descriptor, you need to make an **analytical comparison of ideas and meanings**. The following extract from a sample answer to Activity 5 would hit the grade A requirement.

Love is shown very differently in these two poems, perhaps reflecting different stages of a relationship. In 'Quickdraw' the other person is full of aggression and armed conflict; her voice fires 'a pellet in my ear', for instance. In 'Hour' the two seem united throughout: the poem is dominated by 'we' rather than 'you' and 'I' – 'we are millionaires'. Time seems to behave differently in each poem, too. 'Quickdraw' moves quickly, sometimes with the speed of a bullet or 'pellet', perhaps reflecting a relationship out of control, whereas in 'Hour' they can 'backhand the night' into arriving more slowly. The titles show the same thing: 'Hour' suggests a length of time, whereas 'Quickdraw' not only suggests something quick, but two words are speedily jammed together into one.

Comparing writers' methods and purposes

Compare how the two writers finish the poems in the last line of each, exploring similarities and differences. Discuss or make notes on:

- the different effects of the repetitions
- how each finishes the sense of the poems
- the differences in punctuation between the two, and the effects they have.

GradeStudio

Sample answer B

To achieve a B on this AO3 descriptor, you need to make a **developed comparison of ideas, meanings and techniques** and show **appreciation of writers' uses of language and/ or structure and/or form and their effects on readers**. The following extract from a sample answer to Activity 6 would hit the grade B requirement.

Both poems end with a line containing a very obvious repetition, but they have very different effects. 'Hour' is about creating something precious from something simple, so each repetition, close together, is like the spinning of a wheel, or one more layer. 'Quickdraw', on the other hand, is destructive, and each 'and this' is like the kiss on the text message, but it is a deadly kiss. The 'gold' repetitions are close together, but 'and this' is divided up so that they are like single blows.

Writing in the exam

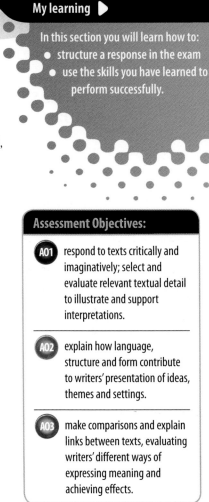

In this section you will learn how to:
- structure a response in the exam
- use the skills you have learned to perform successfully.

Writing your response – planning and structuring

When faced with any exam question your approach should be: Read, Think, Write, Edit.

Read

Read the questions and choose quickly which one to answer based on the poem that is named, or on what each question is asking you to do.

Think

This is the planning stage so don't start writing straight away. Think about the question carefully first! The first word of the exam task is likely to be 'compare' so you should build your response around a comparison of the two poems. You should establish a comparative framework such as the one on page 118 before you write. Within it, jot down ideas from the poems, and one or two details that you're planning to use. Choose things that you can write quite a lot about.

This whole process should take no more than 5 minutes (and not less than 2) as you only have 45 minutes for the whole task.

Write

When you write, you must show: what you think about the poems; why they are written in the ways they are; and what happens when you compare the poems, or parts of them (i.e. the things the Assessment Objectives focus on). The phrase 'or parts of them' is important. Don't write everything you know about the poems. Instead, select from what you know to write about the poems in a way that answers the question.

Edit

If you have any time left, you should look for ways to improve your answer. Could you add another meaning of a word or phrase? Is there another effect of a writer's choice of language? Additions of this kind might gain an extra mark.

Assessment Objectives:

AO1 respond to texts critically and imaginatively; select and evaluate relevant textual detail to illustrate and support interpretations.

AO2 explain how language, structure and form contribute to writers' presentation of ideas, themes and settings.

AO3 make comparisons and explain links between texts, evaluating writers' different ways of expressing meaning and achieving effects.

Putting it into practice

Let's take a typical exam question:

Compare (AO3) the ways in which parents (AO1) are presented in 'Praise Song for My Mother' and one other poem from 'Relationships' (AO2).

Let's suppose that you chose 'Harmonium' as a good choice to compare with 'Praise Song for My Mother' – both are about parents from the point of view of a child, both have similar feelings about the parent, though in some ways they're different, and the methods they use are very different.

First, you need to jot down a few ideas from the poems that you're going to use when you write. There are lots of ways of doing this, but something like the spider diagram below would work:

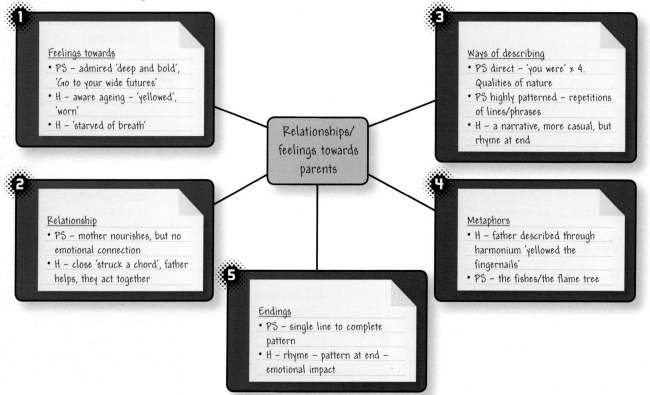

1

Feelings towards
- PS – admired 'deep and bold', 'Go to your wide futures'
- H – aware ageing – 'yellowed', 'worn'
- H – 'starved of breath'

2

Relationship
- PS – mother nourishes, but no emotional connection
- H – close 'struck a chord', father helps, they act together

Relationships/ feelings towards parents

3

Ways of describing
- PS direct – 'you were' x 4. Qualities of nature
- PS highly patterned – repetitions of lines/phrases
- H – a narrative, more casual, but rhyme at end

4

Metaphors
- H – father described through harmonium 'yellowed the fingernails'
- PS – the fishes/the flame tree

5

Endings
- PS – single line to complete pattern
- H – rhyme – pattern at end – emotional impact

In the notes above, the student decided that the feelings towards the parents in each poem and the relationships could be quite similar, but the poems were different in method, so the rest of the response could be structured around different methods. The ideas here are enough: the task is not to try to offer an exhaustive account – you are just showing off your thinking and writing skills.

After thinking of these five different things, the student jotted down some relevant notes, and then decided what order to write in (indicated by the numbers). The student decided that the endings might make a good last paragraph because they offered the chance to write a lot about a little at the end. The rest of the headings could probably be dealt with in one paragraph each.

GradeStudio

Read the extracts from these sample student answers, together with the question below and the examiner comments. You could then try the sample exam question at the end.

Compare the ways in which parents are presented in 'Praise Song for My Mother' and one other poem from 'Relationships'.

Openings

B grade answer

Student A

The feelings towards the parents in the poems seem to be quite similar, in the sense that they are looking affectionately at a parent in the past. 'Harmonium' switches to the present in the last stanza, though, and the affection is different. The speaker, describing his father through the harmonium, is aware of his ageing, shown in 'yellowed' and 'worn'. He is moved by the idea of his father's death, as he is 'starved of breath' at the thought. In 'Praise Song' the speaker admires her mother for being 'deep and bold' and for her unselfishness in saying 'Go to your wide futures'. She is not moved in the same way as in 'Harmonium', though.

Examiner comment

Student A is already showing a **developed comparison** of ideas (18–24, equivalent to a grade B).

A* grade answer

Student B

The daughter in 'Praise Song' clearly admires her mother deeply, as she sees all the qualities of nature in her, in warm, strong, universal terms. The son in 'Harmonium' sees nothing like this. Through describing the harmonium, the reader makes the connection with the father, and sees physical qualities, not universal or character traits: it is 'yellowed' and 'worn'. Similarly, the daughter is grateful for her mother's release of her, in general terms: 'Go to your wide futures, you said', whereas the father's help is practical: 'he comes to help me cart it away.' The reader can imply the daughter's gratitude, but the son's emotion at the thought of his father's death is much clearer, as he is too 'starved of breath' to speak. He, and the reader, are more moved by this than by gratitude.

Examiner comment

Student B achieves both **exploration of ideas/themes** and **analytical comparison** (25–30, equivalent to a grade A) in the first four sentences. The final two sentences move to **evaluative comparison** (31–36, equivalent to a grade A*).

Examiner comment

Both students get on with the task straight away, without any need for a generalised opening paragraph.

119

GradeStudio

A paragraph on a device

B grade answer

Student A

Both poems use metaphors. The first three stanzas of 'Harmonium' describe the harmonium, but are also a metaphor for the speaker's father, who is 'due to be bundled off to the skip' with 'yellowed fingernails'. The metaphors in 'Praise Song' are more direct, but much more exotic: 'the moon's eye', 'sunrise', 'the fishes red gill'. The metaphors in 'Harmonium' also include togetherness, while those in 'Praise Song' do not: 'its hummed harmonics still struck a chord'.

Examiner comment

In Student A's response, the two ideas offered hit **developed comparison of ideas, meanings and techniques** (18–24, equivalent to a grade B).

A grade answer

Student B

Both poems use metaphors. The first three stanzas of 'Harmonium' describe the harmonium, but are also a metaphor for the speaker's father, who is 'due to be bundled off to the skip' with 'yellowed fingernails'. The language here is direct, in tune with the rest of the poem, and might seem almost heartless: 'bundled off' and 'skip' apply to rubbish, almost shockingly to the reader who recognises the parallel with the father. The metaphors in 'Praise Song' are more direct, but much more exotic: 'the moon's eye', 'sunrise', 'the fishes red gill' are words that would not belong in the world of 'Harmonium'. The metaphors in 'Harmonium' also include togetherness, while those in 'Praise Song' do not: 'its hummed harmonics still struck a chord': the 'harmonics' are what join the father and son, and the single sound of the 'chord'.

Examiner comment

Student B's response is built around the same ideas, but simply finds more to say about the details. There is **analysis of language** (25–30, equivalent to a grade A) on 'bundled' and 'skip' with a sense of **evaluation**, and **analytical use of detail** (25–30, equivalent to a grade A) in the last sentence.

A paragraph comparing two details

B grade answer

Student A

The endings of the poems are very different. 'Praise Song' is a poem full of patterns: 'you were' is repeated four times, with three and four lines following, building to a single isolated line in 'Go to your wide futures, you said', so that it feels like a summary of the poem, and the mother. There are no such patterns in 'Harmonium', which seems much more casual. It does finish with a full rhyme, though, unlike 'Praise Song'.

Examiner comment

Student A **explains the effect** of the single line (12–17, equivalent to a grade C), and then creates a **developed comparison of writers' uses of form** (18–24, equivalent to a grade B).

A* grade answer

Student B

The endings of the poems are very different. Nichols' poem is highly patterned, using the senses and the elements of nature schematically, repeating participles ('fathoming' etc.) within a repeated pattern of three stanzas, followed by a stanza that has three qualities, a word repeated twice, and a culminating line of one sentence. Armitage's poem appears almost casual by comparison, with much less heightened diction, lines that approximate speech, and just some half-rhymes and chimes. He ends with pattern, as the last two lines form a rhyming couplet to describe harmony between the father and son, in the shape of the son's anticipated grief. He cannot speak the words, but the reader can hear the grief. The reader might admire Nichols' technique, as she admires her mother, but Armitage moves the reader in a way that she does not attempt.

Examiner comment

Student B is highly **analytical** about method, and ends with a highly **evaluative view of the effects and purposes of the writing** (31–36, equivalent to a grade A*).

You are now ready to tackle an exam question. Here's one to try:

Compare the attitudes of the speakers in 'To His Coy Mistress' and 'The Farmer's Bride'.

When you've written your answer, you could mark it, or get a partner to mark it, using the mark scheme on page 134.

My learning ▶

In this section you will learn how to:
- read an unseen poem
- annotate an unseen poem
- write successfully in the exam on the unseen poem.

Assessment Objectives:

AO1 respond to texts critically and imaginatively; select and evaluate relevant textual detail to illustrate and support interpretations.

AO2 explain how language, structure and form contribute to writers' presentation of ideas, themes and settings.

What to look for when reading and annotating an unseen poem

Introduction

Section B in the exam asks you to respond to an unseen poem – one that you have not prepared beforehand.

In this chapter of the book you will be:

▶ learning how to read the unseen poem in the examination

▶ learning how to annotate it before you write

▶ learning how to write successfully

▶ practising exam-style questions.

The skills you need to show are the same ones you worked on in thinking and writing about the poems you studied for Section A of the exam. The two Assessment Objectives tested are the same as those in Section A, so you should be familiar with these from the poems you have studied. You don't have to compare in Section B, so AO3 isn't present here. You have 30 minutes in the exam to answer the question on the unseen poem, and you have to think within this time before you start to write.

Reading the poem – what to look for

The Assessment Objectives ask you to do two things:

1 Say what you think the poem is about overall, what the poet has to say, and how these ideas and meanings are shown in the poem.

2 Say how the writer has written the poem to convey these ideas to the reader.

The two questions you will be asked about the poem are about exactly these things, so they are what you should look for when you read the poem.

Here is a list of questions to ask yourself as you read the unseen poem, which will help you to respond to the exam question.

1 What is this poem about as a whole, and what ideas are being expressed?

For example, the poem might be about a person, or a place, and might express ideas about the person or the place as the poem goes on. The ideas might develop as the poem unfolds, or just give some isolated pictures. The poem might be about an event, and might have things to say about what happened.

2 How do the details of the poem create the ideas and meanings that you've found?

This might start with the title, and then be found in words, phrases and so on through the poem. If it is a descriptive poem, the writer might have used the senses in their writing. You don't have to write about every line of the poem in the exam, but you do have to use details from the poem to support what you say.

3 How does the writer use language to help convey what he or she has to say?

There's a whole range of devices which a writer might have used in writing the poem. You might find repetition, or figures of speech like **similes** or **metaphors**, or sounds like **alliteration**, or **assonance**, and so on. Whatever you find, remember that there is little point in just identifying it: you need to have an idea of why the writer is using a device.

4 How does the writer use structure to help convey what he or she has to say?

The writer might have built up the poem in stages towards the ending, or used different times like past and present, and so on.

5 How does the writer use form to help convey what he or she has to say?

The writer might have used **rhyme** or **rhythm** in a particular way, or spread words across lines (**enjambment**), or used a lot of **end-stopped lines** for a particular effect. Again, remember that the effect is what you have to think about. Just saying 'this poem uses rhyme,' for instance, would not get you any marks.

6 What is your response to the poem?

When you have looked at the poem carefully you might well have a view about the poem – what you think about what is being said, and how successful you think the writing is. Don't be afraid to use this when you write – it's often a way of achieving higher marks.

Reading and annotating an unseen poem

Having read the guidance on the previous two pages on what to look for in an unseen poem, you are now going to put this into action in a particular poem.

Read the poem below several times, then complete Activity 1 opposite.

> **Poem Glossary**
>
> **a skittle of milk** children in school used to receive free milk every day
>
> **Brady and Hindley** the 'Moors murderers', two notorious child-murderers in the 1960s
>
> **Tana, Ethiopia, Khartoum and Aswân** places on the map they are following

In Mrs Tilscher's Class

Carol Ann Duffy

You could travel up the Blue Nile
with your finger, tracing the route
while Mrs Tilscher chanted the scenery.
Tana. Ethiopia. Khartoum. Aswân.
That for an hour, then a skittle of milk
and the chalky Pyramids rubbed into dust.
A window opened with a long pole.
The laugh of a bell swung by a running child.

This was better than home. Enthralling books.
The classroom glowed like a sweet shop.
Sugar paper. Coloured shapes. Brady and Hindley
faded, like the faint, uneasy smudge of a mistake.
Mrs Tilscher loved you. Some mornings, you found
she'd left a good gold star by your name.
The scent of a pencil slowly, carefully, shaved.
A xylophone's nonsense heard from another form.

Over the Easter term, the inky tadpoles changed
from commas into exclamation marks. Three frogs
hopped in the playground, freed by a dunce,
followed by a line of kids, jumping and croaking
away from the lunch queue. A rough boy
told you how you were born. You kicked him, but stared
at your parents, appalled, when you got back home.

That feverish July, the air tasted of electricity.
A tangible alarm made you always untidy, hot,
fractious under the heavy, sexy sky. You asked her
how you were born and Mrs Tilscher smiled,
then turned away. Reports were handed out.
You ran through the gates, impatient to be grown,
as the sky split open into a thunderstorm.

Using the questions on pages 122 and 123 as a guide, list as many relevant points as you can find in the poem 'In Mrs Tilscher's Class'.

You could:
* start with what you think the poem is about
* then think about the way it's written.

Or you could do it the other way round, starting by noticing things like **rhyme** or **metaphors**.

Remember that you do need to do both these things to get as many marks as you can – saying what it's about without looking at technique is only half an answer, and writing about techniques without showing exactly how they deliver meaning and effect is only half an answer.

Possible answers

In the exam, as you find things, you should pick them out in the poem, by underlining, circling, or making quick marginal notes. These annotations will form the basis of what you are going to write. Here are some of the things you might have noticed in reading 'In Mrs Tilscher's Class' several times and attempting Activity 1.

1   The title says a lot about the poem here – it is about education, in the sense that it's in a 'class', and 'Mrs Tilscher' is a primary-school teacher. There are a lot of details about the classroom, and about Mrs Tilscher, who was clearly admired by the child at the centre of the story. The poem seems to be about growing up, too – the child is 'impatient to be grown' at the end of the poem.

2   The child's love for Mrs Tilscher and her classroom is clear in the second verse. Words here include 'better', 'enthralling', 'loved' and 'good'. The senses are used heavily in the last three lines – the appearance, smell and sound of the classroom. The second half has ideas about getting older, after the word 'changed'. Parents are seen in a different way, and the child is aware of it in the last verse, as shown by the words 'feverish', 'sexy', 'impatient'. The last line seems to suggest a threatening change.

3   The **diction** of this poem – the type of words and phrases that are used – suggests a child's language, even though the point of view is of an adult looking back. 'You could travel', 'a good gold star'. The **imagery** describes childish enjoyment – 'the laugh of a bell', 'glowed like a sweet shop'.

4   The poem changes in the middle: the first two verses show enjoyment; the 'changed' in the first line of the third verse marks a shift to uneasiness, then 'alarm'. The last line is a complete contrast to the first.

5   The key moment of the poem is emphasised by 'changed' at the end of a line – lifted out by the pause that follows.

If you had annotated this poem in the exam, this is what it might have looked like if you had seen the things listed on the previous page.

In Mrs Tilscher's Class

Children's point of view – 'you could': diction

You could travel up the Blue Nile
with your finger, tracing the route
while Mrs Tilscher chanted the scenery.
Tana. Ethiopia. Khartoum. Aswân.
That for an hour, then a skittle of milk
and the chalky Pyramids rubbed into dust.
A window opened with a long pole.

Metaphor/ enjoyment

The laugh of a bell swung by a running child.
This was better than home. Enthralling books.
The classroom glowed like a sweet shop. — Simile – child's view
Sugar paper. Coloured shapes. Brady and Hindley

Safety

faded, like the faint, uneasy smudge of a mistake.
Mrs Tilscher loved you. Some mornings, you found
she'd left a good gold star by your name.

Senses: sight, smell, sound

The scent of a pencil slowly, carefully, shaved.
A xylophone's nonsense heard from another form.
Over the Easter term, the inky tadpoles changed — End of line

Length

from commas into exclamation marks. Three frogs
hopped in the playground, freed by a dunce,
followed by a line of kids, jumping and croaking
away from the lunch queue. A rough boy
told you how you were born. You kicked him, but stared
at your parents, appalled, when you got back home.
That feverish July, the air tasted of electricity. — Sense
A tangible alarm made you always untidy, hot,
fractious under the heavy, sexy sky. You asked her
how you were born and Mrs Tilscher smiled,
then turned away. Reports were handed out.— End of year

Suggests growing up

You ran through the gates, impatient to be grown,
as the sky split open into a thunderstorm.

Threatening change

Writing a response in the exam

My learning ▶

In this section you will learn:
- how to write successfully in the exam on the unseen poem
- what different levels of student response look like.

Writing in the exam

If 'In Mrs Tilscher's Class' appeared on the exam paper (which it won't!), the question you might be asked to answer could be:

What does the poem say about the speaker's childhood experience, and how does the writer show what she thinks and feels?

You will have 30 minutes to do this whole task, so the examiner will not expect you to be writing a huge amount. Just like the poems you have to respond to in Section A, you are not expected to show that you understand every line of the poem, or to tell the 'story' of the whole thing by going through it from the beginning to the end. Rather, you have to use some details from the poem to show what skills you have learned about reading and writing about poetry, in line with the Assessment Objectives.

So, you can afford to spend 5–10 minutes thinking about what's on the page, and annotating it as demonstrated opposite, so that you're ready to start writing. This will allow you to develop an overview of the poem before you start to write, instead of just starting to write about an isolated feature of the poem.

For example, 'This poem is about a child's memory of primary school, but it is also about the disturbing changes that happen to a child at this age' would be a much better start than 'The writer uses metaphors like the laugh of a bell'.

You are left with 20–25 minutes to respond to the two questions, so concentrate on these and on using your annotations, though you might find more things to say as you write.

On the following two pages are sample student answers with examiner comments to the question on 'In Mrs Tilscher's Class' above. Read these, then have a go at a question on a new poem on the pages that follow.

GradeStudio

The poem these students have looked at is 'In Mrs Tilscher's Class' on page 124. The question they are responding to is:

What does the poem say about the speaker's childhood experience, and how does the writer show what she thinks and feels?

B grade answer

Student A

This poem is about a child's memory of her primary school, but it is also about the disturbing changes that happen to a child at this age. It is obvious that the child loved her teacher, and the classroom – it was 'better than home' and the books were 'enthralling'. It was a place of safety, too – inside the class the idea of the murderers 'faded', though the child is still aware of them, shown by 'uneasy'. This feeling becomes much clearer in the second half of the poem, when things 'changed'. The child is 'appalled', full of 'alarm' and 'impatient', though still a child, as you can tell from 'ran through the gates'.

thoughtful consideration of ideas

qualified response

details linked

Carol Ann Duffy uses childlike words and phrases throughout the poem to convey the child's point of view, even though it is also the point of view of an adult looking back. You can see this from 'You could travel up the Blue Nile/with your finger', and from 'the classroom glowed like a sweet shop', which catches the kind of thing a child would enjoy. 'Sugar paper' cleverly combines the idea of the sweet shop and the contents of the classroom through the word 'sweet'.

explanation of effect

appreciation of writer's use of language

Examiner comment

Although this response is not very long, it covers all of the 10–12 criteria. The attraction of the classroom is quickly established, but then another aspect of it is introduced – hitting a 10–12 descriptor, **thoughtful consideration**. **Details are linked** carefully to the idea of 'changed', ranging through the poem, and then there is the **qualification** 'though still a child'. The second paragraph deals with diction and metaphor, **explaining clearly the effect** of 'like a sweet shop', and the additional comment on the two effects of 'sugar' shows **appreciation of language**. The response only deals with language, not form or structure, but that is not a problem. The mark scheme descriptor says 'and/or'. The response gains 12 marks (equivalent to a grade B).

A* grade answer

Student B

This poem is about a child's memory of her primary school, but it is also about the disturbing changes that happen to a child at this age, marked by the huge swing of emotions in the poem. The poem begins quietly enough, with a mostly factual first verse: only the 'laugh of a bell' directly suggests motion, and is not connected to the speaker. 'Enthralling' and 'loved' continue that feeling, but with the 'uneasy smudge' of the Moors murderers striking a first uneasy note. The dramatic change comes at the beginning of the third verse. The reader feels the shift sharply with the placement of 'changed' at the end of the line, and visually in the middle of the poem, and especially in the change from 'commas' to 'exclamation marks'. At first sight this is just an indication of growth and length, but the shape of the marks tells another story: 'commas' suggests the shape of a foetus, perhaps, of humans as well as frogs, whereas the exclamation mark both stands tall with the onset of adulthood and implies the drama to come after the stability of the classroom.

> insightful exploratory response

> close analysis of detail

The writer conveys the child's state of mind through lavish use of the senses. In the first half of the poem it is innocent, with the last three lines of the second verse 'slowly, carefully' detailing sight, smell and sound. In the final verse, though, this has become oppressive – 'feverish', 'sexy' and 'hot' and the sky 'tasted of electricity'. This build-up explodes at the end of the poem. The sense of change is marked with 'reports were handed out,' an end-of-year moment, and then the penultimate line underlines change with every word. The urgency of 'ran' is a stark contrast to the slow movement of the finger at the beginning, and 'through the gates' suggests more than the literal escape from school: attached to 'impatient to be grown', it suggests a child ready to burst through the bonds of the child's world. The last line dramatises the end of childhood with the sound and fury of a storm, both threatening and immediate, as suggested by 'split'.

> evaluation of use of language

> convincing interpretation of ideas

Examiner comment

The first sentence this time marks a writer who knows where the response is going, as the 'huge swing of emotions' is what is dealt with in the rest of the response. The response works very closely on 'commas into exclamation marks', showing an **insightful exploratory response** and **close analysis** of detail. The second paragraph also has a sense of dealing with the whole poem's impact, and how this is achieved. Again, the response dwells on a small part, the last two lines of the poem, and in doing so hits **evaluation of language** in 'ran through the gates', and **convincing interpretation** of the last line. The response has hit all the 16–18 descriptors, so achieves 18 marks (equivalent to a grade A*).

Here are two more poems for you to work on. You could do the first one with a partner, and try the second one yourself. You could mark both using the mark scheme on page 136.

using the mark scheme on page 136.

Activity 2

Read the poem below, then complete the following question.

What do you think the poet wants the reader to think about the jaguar, and how does he present the animal by the ways he writes?

If you want to time yourself, in the exam you should spend around 30 minutes on this question.

▶ **Poem Glossary**

jaguar a large wild cat, a bit like a leopard

indolence laziness, doing nothing

The Jaguar

Ted Hughes

The apes yawn and adore their fleas in the sun.
The parrots shriek as if they were on fire, or strut
Like cheap tarts to attract the stroller with the nut.
Fatigued with indolence, tiger and lion

Lie still as the sun. The boa-constrictor's coil
Is a fossil. Cage after cage seems empty, or
Stinks of sleepers from the breathing straw.
It might be painted on a nursery wall.

But who runs like the rest past these arrives
At a cage where the crowd stands, stares, mesmerized,
As a child at a dream, at a jaguar hurrying enraged
Through prison darkness after the drills of his eyes

On a short fierce fuse. Not in boredom –
The eye satisfied to be blind in fire,
By the bang of blood in the brain deaf the ear –
He spins from the bars, but there's no cage to him

More than to the visionary his cell:
His stride is wildernesses of freedom:
The world rolls under the long thrust of his heel.
Over the cage floor the horizons come.

Read the poem below, then complete the following question.

What do you think is the nature of the mirror and the woman in the poem, and how does the poet present them by the ways she writes?

If you want to time yourself, in the exam you should spend around 30 minutes on this question.

Mirror

Sylvia Plath

I am silver and exact. I have no preconceptions.
Whatever I see I swallow immediately
Just as it is, unmisted by love or dislike.
I am not cruel, only truthful –
The eye of the little god, four cornered.
Most of the time I meditate on the opposite wall.
It is pink, with speckles. I have looked at it so long
I think it is a part of my heart. But it flickers.
Faces and darkness separate us over and over.

Now I am a lake. A woman bends over me,
Searching my reaches for what she really is.
Then she turns to those liars, the candles or the moon.
I see her back, and reflect it faithfully.
She rewards me with tears and an agitation of hands.
I am important to her. She comes and goes.
Each morning it is her face that replaces the darkness.
In me she has drowned a young girl, and in me an old woman
Rises toward her day after day, like a terrible fish.

Unit 2 Poetry across time – Sample Higher Tier exam paper

Section A: Anthology

This section relates to the AQA Anthology that you have been using during the course.

Answer one question from this section on the poems you have studied in the Anthology.

You are advised to spend about 45 minutes on this section.

Relationships

EITHER

Question 1

Compare how children are presented in 'Nettles' and **one** other poem from 'Relationships'.

OR

Question 2

Compare how love is presented in 'To His Coy Mistress' and **one** other poem from 'Relationships'.

(36 marks)

Conflict

EITHER

Question 3

Compare how the results of conflict are shown in 'Mametz Wood' and **one** other poem from 'Conflict'.

OR

Question 4

Compare how language is used to present ideas in 'Belfast Confetti' and **one** other poem from 'Conflict'.

(36 marks)

Place

EITHER

Question 5

Compare how feelings are presented in 'Crossing the Loch' and **one** other poem from 'Place'.

OR

Question 6

Compare how memory is presented in 'Cold Knap Lake' and **one** other poem from 'Place'.

(36 marks)

Character and voice

EITHER

Question 7

Compare how a voice is created in 'My Last Duchess' and **one** other poem from 'Character and voice'.

OR

Question 8

Compare how a relationship is presented in 'Medusa' and **one** other poem from 'Character and voice'.

(36 marks)

Section B: Unseen Poetry

Answer the question in this section.

You are advised to spend about 30 minutes on this section.

Read the poem below, and answer the question that follows.

The Poacher

Turning aside, never meeting
In the still lanes, fly infested,
Our frank greeting with quick smile,
You are the wind that set the bramble
Aimlessly clawing the void air.
The fox knows you, the sly weasel
Feels always the steel comb
Of eyes parting like sharp rain
Among the grasses its smooth fur.
No smoke haunting the cold chimney
Over your hearth betrays your dwelling
In blue writing above the trees.
The robed night, your dark familiar,
Covers your movements; the slick sun,
A dawn accomplice, removes your tracks
One by one from the bright dew.

R.S. Thomas

Question 9

How does the writer present the character of the poacher in the poem?

(18 marks)

Mark schemes

Section A mark scheme

Below is the mark scheme for Section A of the Poetry unit.

A* 31–36 marks	**In response to the task, candidates demonstrate:** • insightful exploratory response to text • close analysis of detail to support interpretation • evaluation of writers' uses of language and/or structure and/or form and their effects on readers • convincing/imaginative interpretation of ideas/themes • evaluative comparison of ideas and/or meanings and/or techniques • evaluative selection of a range of telling detail integrated into comparison
A 25–30 marks	**In response to the task, candidates demonstrate:** • exploratory response to text • analytical use of detail to support interpretation • analysis of writers' uses of language and/or structure and/or form and their effects on readers • exploration of ideas/themes • analytical comparison of ideas and/or meanings and/or techniques • selection of a range of telling details as the basis for comparison
B 18–24 marks	**In response to the task, candidates demonstrate:** • considered/qualified response to text • details linked to interpretation • appreciation/consideration of writers' uses of language and/or structure and/or form and their effects on readers • thoughtful consideration of ideas/themes • developed comparison of ideas and/or meanings and/or techniques • thoughtful selection and consideration of material for comparison
C 12–17 marks	**In response to the task, candidates demonstrate:** • sustained response to elements of text • effective use of details to support interpretation • explanation of effect(s) of writers' uses of language and/or structure and/or form and their effects on readers • appropriate comment on ideas/themes • sustained focus on similarities/differences in ideas and/or meanings and/or techniques • selection of material for a range of comparisons
D 6–11 marks	**In response to the task, candidates demonstrate:** • explained response to element(s) of text • details used to support a range of comments • identification of effect(s) of writers' choices of language and/or structure and/or form intended/achieved • awareness of feelings/attitudes/meanings • structured comments on similarities/differences in ideas and/or meanings and/or techniques • selection of material to support structured comparative comment
E 1–5 marks	**In response to the task, candidates demonstrate:** • supported response to text • details used to support points/comments • awareness of writers making choice(s) of language and/or structure and/or form • generalisation(s) about ideas/themes • some comments comparing ideas and/or meanings and/or techniques • selection of some details for comparison

This is exactly the mark scheme that examiners use. Below you will find what some of the terms mean, and how you use the scheme to get to a mark.

What do the words in the mark scheme mean?

E
- 'supported response to text'. This is a response to the text supported with a detail or a quotation from the poem.
- 'some comments comparing' means isolated comments comparing, but not in a structured or sustained way.

D
- 'identification of effects'. This describes a comment that says what effect a particular device has, without explaining <u>how</u> it has that effect. Explaining would move it into Band 4.
- 'structured comments on similarities/differences' usually describes a passage comparing poems, or details from poems, in more than one way.

C
- 'sustained response to' describes a passage of writing about an element of the text, such as character or ideas, which covers several points. It could just be a paragraph rather than the whole response.
- Similarly, 'sustained focus on similarities/differences' describes a response which has comparison in mind all the time, though of course not every sentence has to be comparative.

B
- Some of the key words here are 'developed', 'considered/qualified' and 'consideration'. They all describe writing that deals with more than one thing, in the sense that one idea follows on or develops from another. 'It means this, but it could mean this as well, and it also implies that ...'.
- A 'developed comparison' probably compares the poems, or details of the poems, but then goes on to compare them in another way that develops the first idea.

A
- 'Analytical' occurs a lot at this level. It describes an idea, a device or a comparison being taken apart and examined carefully. 'Exploratory' describes an approach that looks at several interpretations or meanings, not just two.

A*
- 'Evaluative' follows on from 'analytical', mostly, it describes the final weighing of effect of an idea, method or comparison.

Using the mark schemes

Using the mark schemes is quite simple, as the number of bullets in each band is the same as the number of marks that can be awarded. So, if a response hits all of the descriptors (bullets) in the 12–17 band and two of the 18–24 band, it is worth 20 marks. If it does one thing in a band above, though, say in the 25–30 band, that can count too. It goes in the place of one that's missing – so now the response gets 3 in the 18–24 band, and is worth 21 marks.

Section B mark scheme

This is the mark scheme the examiner will use to mark your answer to the Unseen Poetry task.

A* 16–18 marks	**In response to the task, candidates demonstrate:** • insightful exploratory response to text • close analysis of detail to support interpretation • evaluation of writers' uses of language and/or structure and/or form and their effects on readers • convincing/imaginative interpretation of ideas/themes
A 13–15 marks	**In response to the task, candidates demonstrate:** • exploratory response to text • analytical use of detail to support interpretation • analysis of writers' uses of language and/or structure and/or form and their effects on readers • exploration of ideas/themes
B 10–12 marks	**In response to the task, candidates demonstrate:** • considered/qualified response to text • details linked to interpretation • appreciation/consideration of writers' uses of language and/or structure and/or form and their effects on readers • thoughtful consideration of ideas/themes
C 7–9 marks	**In response to the task, candidates demonstrate:** • sustained response to elements of text • effective use of details to support interpretation • explanation of effect(s) of writers' uses of language and/or structure and/or form and their effects on readers • appropriate comment on ideas/themes
D 4–6 marks	**In response to the task, candidates demonstrate:** • explained response to element(s) of text • details used to support a range of comments • identification of effect(s) of writers' choices of language and/or structure and/or form intended/achieved • awareness of ideas/themes
E 1–3 marks	**In response to the task, candidates demonstrate:** • supported response to text • details used to support points/comments • awareness of writers making choice(s) of language and/or structure and/or form • generalisation(s) about ideas/themes

Glossary of Poetic Devices

alliteration   the deliberate repetition of consonant sounds at the beginning of words to gain a particular effect, e.g. 'and handle and hold' (The Manhunt)

assonance   the deliberate repetition of vowel sounds to gain a particular effect, e.g. 'tipples over' and 'spills down' (Storm in the Black Forest)

context   something outside the text that affects its meaning, such as:

▶ historical context, e.g. the Chernobyl incident in 'Neighbours'

▶ social context, e.g. nineteenth-century city conditions in 'London'

▶ language context, e.g. dialect in 'Hard Water', 'Singh Song'

dialect words   words from a particular region, e.g. 'mardy' (Hard Water)

diction   the choice of words used, e.g. formal or informal words

dramatic monologue   a poem supposedly spoken by a character, e.g. 'My Last Duchess'

end-stopped lines   lines of verse that end with a full stop, e.g. the last four lines of 'Hawk Roosting'

enjambment   the continuation of a sentence or phrase from one line into the next without a pause, e.g. 'and so forth oh/say can you see' (next to of course god America)

form   general way of organising a poem, e.g. rhyme, rhythm, etc. There are some particular forms such as ballads and sonnets

half-rhyme   words in which the consonants rhyme rather than the vowels, e.g. 'seeds/sides' (Futility)

iambic pentameter   a line of verse with five beats, which fall on the second syllable of each pair, e.g. 'Which alters when it alteration finds' (Sonnet 116)

imagery   language in a poem which conjures up an idea for the reader from one of the five senses. Specific forms of imagery include metaphors and similes

metaphor   an image which makes an implied comparison by stating that something is the thing it resembles, e.g. 'The tent of the hills' (Wind)

non-standard English   a variety of English other than standard, e.g. Caribbean English in 'Checking Out Me History'

personification   a device whereby an abstract concept or non-living thing is represented as having human characteristics, e.g. 'Old Father Time'

refrain   a recurring phrase or lines at the end of each verse of poetry, like a chorus, e.g. 'Brendon Gallacher' (Brendon Gallacher)

rhyme   the repetition of a vowel sound, usually in words at the end of lines, for example:

'I'm one of your talking wounded.
I'm a hostage. I'm maroonded.' (In Paris with You)
These can also be an internal rhyme, when a vowel sound is repeated within a line, such as 'rouse' and 'now' in this line from 'Futility':
'If anything might rouse him now'

rhyme scheme   the way rhymes within a poem are organised

rhyming couplets   two lines following one another which rhyme, e.g. 'word/heard' in the last two lines of 'Harmonium'

rhythm   the arrangement of words to form a regular beat through a pattern of stresses, e.g. 'The lone and level sands stretch far away' (Ozymandias)

simile   a comparison between two things, using 'like' or 'as', e.g. 'crowed like a rooster' (Cameo Appearance)

sonnet   a poem of fourteen lines, usually ending with a rhyming couplet, e.g. 'next to of course god America' (though this is a variation on a sonnet)

speaker   the 'voice' who is speaking in a poem written in the first person, e.g. the Duke in 'My Last Duchess'

stanza   a clearly demarcated part of a poem

structure   how the author has organised his/her work into patterns. Some fixed-form poems like sonnets have fixed structures of rhyme etc., but a poem might have structure in the way it is organised into stanzas, or what they open and close with, or where a particular word or idea is placed

symbol   something used to stand for or represent something else, e.g. the flag representing nationalism in 'Flag'

tone   the overall feeling or mood of a poem, e.g. the sorrowful tone of 'The Falling Leaves'

Heinemann is an imprint of Pearson Education Limited, a company incorporated in England and Wales, having its registered office at Edinburgh Gate, Harlow, Essex CM20 2JE. Registered company number: 872828

www.pearsonschools.co.uk

Heinemann is a registered trademark of Pearson Education Limited

Text © Pearson Education Limited

First published 2010

14 13 12 11 10
10 9 8 7 6 5 4 3 2 1

British Library Cataloguing in Publication Data

A catalogue record for this book is available from the British Library.

ISBN 978 0 435118 50 1

Edited by Jane Anson
Designed by Wooden Ark Studios
Typeset by Kamae Design, Oxford
Original illustrations © Pearson Education Limited 2010
Illustrated by Leo Brown and Kamae Design
Cover design by Wooden Ark Studios
Picture research by Sally Cole Picture Research
Cover photo © Bill Brooks/Masterfile
Printed and bound in the UK by Scotprint

Acknowledgements

The author and publisher would like to thank the following individuals and organisations for permission to reproduce photographs:

Bob Krist/Corbis pp. 2, 14; Laurence Monneret/Stone/Getty Images pp. 5, 11; Bettmann/Corbis p. 6; Toussaint l'Ouverture François Dominique, Haitian freedom fighter, the "black Napoleon". Breda (Haiti) 20.5.1743 - Fort Joux near Besançon 7.4.1803. AKG p. 7; Pernilla Zetterman/Etsa/Corbis p. 8; Louis Moses/zefa/Corbis p. 10; Gary Salter/Corbis p. 12; Mary Evans p. 13; Bronzino, Agnolo (1503–1572), school: portrait of Lucrezia di Cosimo 1. Florence, Galleria degli Uffizi © 1990. Photo Scala, Florence – courtesy of the Ministero Beni Att. Culturali p. 15; Aida Ricciardiello/Shutterstock p. 16; Robert Dowling/Corbis p. 17; reproduced with permission of Punch Ltd, www.Punch.co.uk p. 18; Hulton Archive/Getty Images p. 19; Carl Purcell/Corbis p. 20; Nimatallah/akg images p. 21; Joanna McCarthy/Photolibrary pp. 32, 50; Ashley Cooper/Corbis pp. 34, 38; Richard Schultz/Corbis pp. 35, 45; Andrew Darrington/Alamy p. 36; Philippe Caron/Sygma/Corbis p. 37; Millais, John Everett 1829–1896. "Ophelia", 1852. (After Shakespeare, Hamlet.) Oil on canvas, 76.2 x 111.8cm. London, Tate Gallery/AKG p. 39; Douglas Peebles/Photolibrary Group p. 40; Sipa Press/Rex Features p. 41; WIN-Initiative/Getty Images p. 42; Jack Andersen/Foodpix/Getty Images p. 43; Museum of London/HIP/TopFoto p. 44; AlaskaStock/Photolibrary Group p. 46; Picavet/Getty Images pp. 47, 51; akg p. 48; Rob Matheson/Corbis p. 49; RaduSighe/Reuters pp. 62, 71; Jeff J. Mitchell UK/Reuters pp. 64, 72; Hulton-Deutsch Collection/Corbis pp. 65, 76; Benelux/Corbis p. 66; Sean Adair/Reuters p. 67; We are making a new World (1918), Paul Nash/Imperial War Museum p. 68; 2006 Alinari/TopFoto pp. 69, 81; reproduced with permission of Imtiaz Dharker p. 70; Pearson Education Ltd Mindstudio p. 73; Tim Spence/Lightshaft Ltd/Photolibrary Group p. 74; Topham/Fotomas p. 75; Kathy Collins/Getty Images p. 77; YOSHITSUGU NISHSGAKI/amanaimages/Corbis p. 78; Jurgen Vogt/Alamy p. 79; Gisela Delpho/Photolibrary p. 80; Karin Smeds/Getty Images pp. 92, 109; Backhuysen, Ludolf 1631–1708. "Storm at a mountainous coast", c. 1675. Oil on canvas, 173.5 x 341cm. Brussels, Musées Royaux des Beaux-Arts/AKG pp. 94, 104; Tony Lilley/Alamy pp. 95, 100; Peter Gridley/Getty Images p. 97; Roger-Viollet/Topfoto pp. 98, 111; Corbis p. 99; J. Richards/Alamy p. 101; Bob Thomas/Getty Images p. 102; Chris Tidmore/Shutterstock p. 103; Mohamed Itani/arcangel-images.com p. 105; Young Woman with Letter and Locket, 1667 (oil on panel) by Netscher, Caspar (1639–84) p. 106; Photolibrary Group p. 107; Hugh Shurley/Corbis p. 108; JLP/Jose L. Pelaez/Corbis p. 110.

The author and publisher would like to thank the following individuals and organisations for permission to reproduce copyright material:

'Clown Punk' from *Tyrannosaurus Rex versus The Corduroy Kid* published by Faber and Faber; 'Checking Out Me History' © 1996 by John Agard reproduced by kind permission of John Agard c/o Caroline Sheldon Literary Agency Limited; 'Horse Whisperer' from *Fear of Thunder* by Andrew Forster, published by Flambard Press © Andrew Forster, 2007.

Used by permission of Flambard Press; 'Medusa' from *The Worlds Wife* by Carol Ann Duffy, published by Picador. Used by permission of Picador, a division of Macmillan Books; 'Singh Song' from *Look We Have Coming to Dover* by Daljit Nagra, published by Faber and Faber; 'Brendan Gallacher' (25 lines) from *Two's Company* by Jackie Kay (Blackie, 1992) Copyright © Jackie Kay, 1992. Used by permission of Penguin Group (UK); 'Give' from *Dead Sea Poems* by Simon Armitage, published by Faber and Faber; 'Les Grands Seigneurs' from *Hare Soup* by Dorothy Molloy published by Faber and Faber; 'The River God' from *New Selected Poems* published by New Direction Books. Used by permission of The Estate of James MacGibbon; 'The Hunchback in the Park' by Dylan Thomas from *The Poems* published by J.M. Dent. © Dylan Thomas. Granted by permission of David Higham Associates; 'Case history: Alison (head injury)' by U A Fanthorpe, from *Collected Poems 1978-2003*, published by Perterloo Poets. © U A Fanthorpe. Used by permission of the Estate of U A Fanthorpe; 'On A Portrait of a Deaf Man' from *Best Loved Poems of John Betjeman* published by John Murray. Used by permission of John Murray and Aitken Alexander Associates; 'The Blackbird of Glanmore' from *District and Circle* by Seamus Heaney, published by Faber and Faber; 'Vision' from *Tyrannosaurus Rex versus The Corduroy Kid* published by Faber and Faber; 'The Moment' by Margaret Atwood from *Eating Fire*, published by Virago, a division of Little Brown. Reproduced with permission of Curtis Brown Ltd. London on behalf of Margaret Atwood. © Margaret Atwood 1998; 'Cold Knap Lake' taken from *Collected Poems* by Gillian Clarke. © Gillian Clarke. Published by Carcanet Press Limited. Used by permission of Carcanet Press; 'Price We Pay for the Sun' from *The Fat Black Woman's Poems* published by Virago. © Grace Nichols, reproduced with permission of Curtis Brown Group Ltd.; 'Neighbours' taken from *Collected Poems* by Gillian Clarke. © Gillian Clarke. Published by Carcanet Press Limited. Used by permission of Carcanet Press; 'Crossing the Loch' from *Jizzen* by Kathleen Jamie. © 1999 Kathleen Jamie. Published Picador. Used by permission of Picador, a division of Macmillan books; 'Hard Water' by Jean Sprackland © 2003. Published by Jonathan Cape. Used by permission of Random House UK; 'Below the Green Corrie' from *The Poems of Norman MacCaig* by Norman MacCaig is reproduced by permission of Polygon, an imprint of Birlinn Ltd. (www.birlinn.co.uk); 'Wind' from *Collected Poems* by Ted Hughes, published by Faber and Faber; 'Flag' from: *Half-Caste and other Poems* by John Agard © 2007. Published by Hodder Arnold; 'You have Picked Me Out' by Simon Armitage is reproduced from *Out of the Blue* (Enitharmon Press © 2008) Used by permission; 'Mametz Wood' from *Skirrid Hill* by Owen Sheers. First published by Seren Books. © 2005 Owen Sheers. Reproduced by permission of the author c/o Rogers, Coleridge & White Ltd., 20 Powis Mews, London W11 1JN; 'The Yellow Palm' taken from Selected Poems by Robert Minhinnick. © Rob Minhinnick. Published by Carcanet Press Limited. Used by permission of Carcanet Press; 'The Right Word' taken from: *Terrorist at my Table* by Imtiaz Dharker. Published by Bloodaxe Books, © 2006. Used by permission; 'At the Border' taken from: *Life for Us* by Choman Hardi. Published by Bloodaxe Books © 2004. Used by permission; 'Belfast Confetti' by Ciaran Carson. Used by kind permission of the author and The Gallery Press, Loughcrew, Oldcastle, County Meath, Ireland from *Collected Poems* © 2008; 'Poppies' by Jane Weir. Used by kind permission of Templar Poetry; 'Bayonet Charge' from *Hawke in the Rain* by Ted Hughes, published by Faber and Faber; 'The Falling Leaves' by Margaret Postgate Cole, used by permission of David Higham Associates; 'Come On, Come Back' from *Not Waving but Drowning* published by Penguin Books. Used by permission of The Estate of James MacGibbon; 'next to of course god america' Copyright 1926, 1954 © 1991 by the Trustees for the E.E. Cummings Trust. Copyright © 1985 by George James Firmage, from COMPLETE POEMS: 1904-1962 BY E.E. Cummings, edited by George J. Firmage. Used by permission of Liverright Publishing Corporation United States and WW Norton, United Kingdom; 'Hawk Roosting' from *Selected Poems* by Ted Hughes, published by Faber and Faber; 'The Manhunt' from *The Not Dead* by Simon Armitage, Published by Pomona Books. Used by permission; 'Hour' from *Rapture* by Carol Ann Duffy, published by Picador. Used by permission of Picador, a division of Macmillan Books; 'In Paris With You' by James Fenton from *Selected Poems* published by Penguin books. Reprinted by permission of United Agents on behalf of: James Fenton; 'Quickdraw' from *Rapture* by Carol Ann Duffy, published by Picador. Used by permission of Picador, a division of Macmillan Books; 'Ghazal' by Mimi Khalvati. Used by kind permission of the poet; 'Brothers' from *Fear of Thunder* by Andrew Forster, published by Flambard Press © Andrew Forster, 2007. Used by permission of Flambard Press; 'Praise Song for My Mother' from *The Fat Black Woman's Poems* published by Virago. © Grace Nichols, reproduced with permission of Curtis Brown Group Ltd.; 'Harmonium' by Simon Armitage © Simon Armitage. Used by permission of David Godwin Associates; 'Nettles' from *New and Collected Poems* by Vernon Scannell. Used by permission of The Estate of Vernon Scannell; 'Born Yesterday' by Philip Larkin, taken from *The Less Deceived* published by The Marvell press; 'In Mrs Tilscher's Class' is taken from *The Other Country* by Carol Ann Duffy published by Anvil Press Poetry in 1990. © Carol Ann Duffy. Used by permission; 'The Jaguar' from *Collected Poems* by Ted Hughes, published by Faber and Faber; 'Mirror' from *Collected Poems* by Sylvia Plath, published by Faber and Faber.

Every effort has been made to contact copyright holders of material reproduced in this book. Any omissions will be rectified in subsequent printings if notice is given to the publishers.